WORTH A THOUSAND WORDS

USING GRAPHIC NOVELS TO TEACH VISUAL AND VERBAL LITERACY

Meryl J. Jaffe, PhD and Talia Hurwich

JB JOSSEY-BASS™
A Wiley Brand

Published by Jossey-Bass
A Wiley Brand
535 Mission Street, 14 FL; San Francisco CA 94105-3253—www.josseybass.com

Jossey-Bass books and products are available through most bookstores. To contact Jossey-Bass directly call our Customer Care Department within the U.S. at 800-956-7739, outside the U.S. at 317-572-3986, or fax 317-572-4002.

Wiley publishes in a variety of print and electronic formats and by print-on-demand. Some material included with standard print versions of this book may not be included in e-books or in print-on-demand. If this book refers to media such as a CD or DVD that is not included in the version you purchased, you may download this material at http://booksupport.wiley.com. For more information about Wiley products, visit www.wiley.com.

Library of Congress Cataloging-in-Publication Data

Names: Jaffe, Meryl, author. | Hurwich, Talia, author.
Title: Worth a thousand words : using graphic novels to teach visual and verbal literacy / Meryl J. Jaffe, Talia Hurwich.
Description: San Francisco, CA : Jossey-Bass, 2018. | Includes bibliographical references and index.
Identifiers: LCCN 2018031311 (print) | LCCN 2018047611 (ebook) | ISBN 9781119394617 (Adobe PDF) | ISBN 9781119394631 (ePub) | ISBN 9781119394327 (pbk.)
Subjects: LCSH: Graphic novels in education. | Visual literacy—Study and teaching.
Classification: LCC LB1044.9.C59 (ebook) | LCC LB1044.9.C59 J35 2018 (print) | DDC 371.33—dc23
LC record available at https://lccn.loc.gov/2018031311

Cover design: Wiley

Cover images: © ivector/Shutterstock;© Fernandodiass/Shutterstock

Printed in the United States of America

FIRST EDITION

PB Printing V10005015_110718

CONTENTS

NOTES OF THANKS

First and foremost, thank you to my incredible family who have so enriched my life: to Adam, who has always supported and enabled us all; to Talia, whose strong insightful voice continues to grow and who took this work to places I never dreamed of; to Leah and to Zev, for your honesty and love; and to my mom, Solange, who read aloud to me whenever I asked (especially when she didn't really want or have time to), and to my dad, Lloyd whom I miss terribly and who introduced me to the world of storytelling. I am grateful for all you have given and continue to give me.

To my agent and dear friend, Judy Hansen, for your insights, your letters of introduction, your encouragement, but most of all for your friendship; to our editor Kate Bradford, whose edits and insights have been spot-on and this book is the better for them; to Annette Dorfman, whose friendship I deeply value and who continues to teach me to calm and open my mind – thank you.

To my dear friends, the authors who've joined me on my journey both professionally and socially and who make graphic novels so easy to write about and teach with – Jennifer Holm and Matthew Holm, Janet Lee, Royden Lepp, Cecile Castellucci, Raina Telgemeier, Nathan Hale, Jonathan Hennessey, Jimmy Gownley, Jeff Smith, Scott McCloud, Gene Luen Yang, Kazu Kibuishi, and Joe Kelly (whose book began my journey), and also those whom I've neglected to mention (due to addled brains and deadlines) and those who are yet to come – thank you.

Finally, but most of all, to all the dedicated teachers, librarians and comic book aficionados who helped pave the way for comics in classrooms and to all of you who have picked up this book in hope of expanding your own classroom tools and techniques – thank you.

I consider myself privileged where the people who inspire me (including my family and students) have become peers and friends.

—With my deepest appreciation, Meryl

My path has been slightly different from my mother's, but many of the sentiments are the same. Many thanks to my family: to Lee for his emotional support, delicious meals, and readiness to pick up some of my household chores as I worked on this project; to my parents, who have pushed me to proudly pursue my interests no matter how unconventional they are (in fact, the stranger, the better); to Zev for being my first partner in crime when it came to graphic novels; and to Leah for her skepticism and ability to keep me honest with myself. Thank you to the teachers and administrators who have taught me how to teach: Maxine Borenstein, Jessica Alyesh, and Elisheva Gould. A special thank you to Christie Pearsall, whose creative integration of acting and literature first convinced me that I can bring my hobbies into the classroom (and the source of our tableau vivant activity). Thank you to all my role models at New York University for your interest and your support of a doctoral candidate intensely fascinated by "the funny books"; to the late Harold Wechsler for his infectious, heartwarming enthusiasm and keen ability to guide me – he is deeply missed; and to Bethamie Horowitz, Camillia Matuk, and Miriam Eisenstein Ebsworth for their continued support as I cobble together a research program to better understand the way this medium can be used. Thank you to all the amazing creators of the graphic novels I've encountered: your insights, creativity, and sheer genius regularly reaffirm why I tried to convince my mother all those years ago. Thank you to my students for being guinea pigs for so many of the lessons teachers will find in this book. Finally, thank you to Kate Bradford: your input and insights have been such a boon. You have made this book possible, you have made it what it is today, and for that I cannot thank you enough.

—**Talia**

PREFACE

This book is a true work of love, the product of years of collaboration, and in need of a couple of confessions as well as the notes of thanks.

My *first confession*. Until fairly recently, I didn't think graphic novels were appropriate for my classroom or for my kids' reading pleasure at home. I wanted my kids to be well-read and to be reading quality prose and classics. Comics in my mind were, charitably, a nice (occasional) recreational retreat. In my defense, the only comics I knew were the ones I grew up with – featuring Archie and Veronica and assorted superheroes and offering formulaic stories with few substantive aspirations. The proliferation of sophisticated graphic novels that we are now witnessing emerged only when my kids were in their teens.

I got something of a jolt when my kids were in high school and college. At that time, I was putting together a book proposal on how to work with kids to develop and enhance literacy when I overheard them talking about attending Comic Con. My kids were (and still are) good students and avid readers. They are as comfortable reading Neil Gaiman as they are Alexandre Dumas, so noticing them take a literary detour into graphic novels naturally drew my attention. I asked them, "If I'm so passionate about literacy and getting kids to read, maybe I should take a closer look at graphic novels?" Their response? "DUH!!!"

So I gave them a challenge: I'd read one graphic novel of their choice and decide. My kids chose wisely. They gave me *I Kill Giants*, by Joe Kelly and J. M. Ken Nimura. It was wonderful – deep, beautifully and sensitively written, with metaphors and thoughtful vocabulary. I was blown away by the maturity and complexity of the narrative and how quickly and completely I was swept into the protagonist's world. Tears literally streamed down my face as I read it.

Which leads me to my *second confession*. This book is not only a work of love for books and literacy, it is a work of love because I co-wrote it with one of those children who helped bring me here, my daughter Talia. I wish for all of you who are reading this the opportunity to take a journey like this with your children someday, where you learn, work, collaborate, and grow – together.

In the meantime, Talia and I hope you enjoy our journey. We hope it gets you thinking as Talia (and her siblings) got me thinking all those years ago. And we hope you keep in touch with us. We will have active websites **www.wiley.com/go/worthathousandwords**, meryljaffe.com, and taliahurwich.com where we will continue to review books and place paired reading suggestions, lesson suggestions, and links for additional resources. The book's Wiley website will also have reproducible worksheets from activities shared in this book as well as a Bonus Resource: an extensive list of over 200 graphic novels along with their summaries, suggested grade level appropriateness, and special notes.

Trying new things is never easy, but they often are enriching and they certainly make life more interesting. Good luck with your journeys, and happy reading!

—**Meryl Jaffe**

ABOUT THE AUTHORS

Meryl Jaffe, PhD, is an author specializing in kid-lit and promoting verbal and visual literacies through the use of comic books, traditional prose texts, and multi-multimedia integration. She is also an instructor for the Johns Hopkins University Center for Talented Youth – where she teaches critical reading, writing, and visual literacy courses. In her spare time she concocts awesome kid-lit stories, hones her drawing and paper-cutting skills, tries to find quality time with husband Adam and kids, loves reading fiction and artsy, informational, and/or interesting books, and loves hearing from teachers, parents, kids, and fans.

Her previous publications include a featured story, "Dramatic Reading," and an online Teacher's Guide published in the Comic Book Legal Defense Fund's *Liberty Annual* for 2014; "Raising a Reader! How Comics and Graphic Novels Can Help Your Kids Learn to Read" (CBLDF, 2013); and *Using Content-Area Graphic Texts for Learning* (Capstone, 2012). She also writes a featured column for the Comic Book Legal Defense Fund, "Using Graphic Novels in Education." Meryl Jaffe began her career as a classroom (K-8) reading teacher and received her PhD in educational and school psychology with research and publications focused on student reading, critical thinking, and literacy skills.

Talia Hurwich is a doctoral candidate and researcher at New York University, specializing in pop culture and literacy in the classroom and looking particularly at using graphic novels and graphic novel adaptations in and out of the ELA, STEM, and Jewish classroom. Previously, she was a middle school teacher and assistant librarian at an independent school in New York City (where she helped to develop the school's graphic novel collection) and a writing instructor and curriculum mentor for the Johns Hopkins University Center for Talented Youth, where she taught critical reading and writing and mentored teaching assistants and first-year instructors. In the time gained by procrastinating work, she reads; spends time with her husband, Lee, and other members of her family; and spins fire.

Talia's previous publications include "Using Graphic Novels to Get Your Kids Interested in Classic Literature" (Pop Culture Classroom, 2018); "Jewish Education Going Graphic: Classroom Strategies for Using Graphic Novels" (HaYidion, 2016), and several academic publications such as "Cognitive processes and collaborative supports for knowledge integration among youth designing games for science learning" (Proceedings of the 13th International Conference for the Learning Sciences, 2018). She has presented on educational panels at Comic Con, the National Council of Teachers of English, the International Literacy Association, and the 2016 NYC Board of Education teacher workshop "Comics in the Classroom."

GRAPHIC NOVELS
FEARS AND FACTS

We begin by recognizing that most parents and educators have very strong feelings about graphic novels and their place in classroom curricula. For some of you, we will be reinforcing and validating many of your assumptions. For others, we hope to if not convince then to at least leave you open to consideration. For all of you, however, we hope to relay innovative tools and lessons to liven up your classrooms, libraries, and curricula.

Our journey together begins with addressing the fears, concerns, and hesitations teachers have expressed to us during our panels and workshops as we've introduced them to graphic novels. More specifically, we begin by debunking the three most commonly given reasons why teachers are reluctant to incorporate graphic novels into their classroom curricula. All three are valid concerns.

Fears

Fear #1: Classics Versus Graphic Novels and the Fear of Losing the Passion for Prose

As members of a panel addressing graphic novels in classrooms a few years ago at the New York Comic Con, we were presented with the following request at the very end of our session, from a man who sat way in the back of our audience-packed room:

"You make good points about what graphic novels can do, and I hate saying this, but all I see is this dystopian future where people are no longer reading books and are instead totally engaging in screens, online interactions, and popular culture. . . .Address this."

This was a challenging request because we don't totally disagree. For us, the classics represent masterful storytelling, and they are as much products of their time as they are timeless works of literature. As teachers, we use them to teach about Western cultural history and as commentaries of the ongoing "human condition." We use them to develop students' mastery of rhetoric, literacy, aesthetic, and analytic skills that will help them to thrive and to act, write, and sound educated at colleges, parties, interviews, and the workplace.

Recognizing these strengths the classics hold, our humble response is that as parents and educators we must work to find places for both classics and graphic novels in our homes, classrooms, and curricula. They offer very different reading experiences that should not necessarily exclude or preclude one another. There is no "right" way to teach nor one perfect tool to teach with because there is no one "typical" student or one "typical" teacher. We all have different strengths, weaknesses, likes, and dislikes. We all think and work differently. And we all come from different backgrounds that shape us. As a result our teaching tools must also reflect that difference. The books we teach with should reflect diversity in format just as they should reflect diversity in genre, characters, and plot. Furthermore, there is no arguing that we live in a changing society and culture. Images and technology are playing increasingly stronger roles in our lives, and as our modes of communication become more complex, we need to ensure that students have proficiency (if not mastery) in not just written but visual media as well.

Our goal in the pages and chapters that follow is to provide you all a plethora of tools, techniques, and resources from which to make your own choices.

Fear #2: Graphic Novels in Curricula and the Fear of Backlash from Parents or Administrators

There are a number of reasons why teachers fear backlash from parents or administrators for using graphic novels in their curricula. Most of the backlash is due to one or more of the preconceived notions outlined in this section and addressed in greater detail in the chapters that follow. In addition to this information, please make sure to take a look at Appendix A. There, we provide you with specific and detailed steps you can take and references and resource materials you can use to help prevent and/or address backlash or challenges you may encounter due to graphic novel (or any reading text) choices.

Many educators fear backlash for using graphic novels . . .

Because they're perceived predominantly as tools for weak or reluctant and/or English language learners. This is probably due to the fact that this was the reason graphic novels were initially introduced into classrooms. And while they *are* outstanding tools for weak, reluctant, and/or English language learners, their value doesn't end there. It merely begins there.

In addition to recognizing the awards kids' graphic novels are receiving as quality children's and teen's literature – including Caldecott and Newbery awards, National Book Awards, and starred reviews from prestigious literary magazines – educators and librarians are finding that today's kids' graphic novels offer strong examples of language use, vocabulary, and storytelling that benefit all kinds of learners. They foster and reinforce attention, memory, sequencing, and higher-order cognitive skills beneficial to all your students in all content-area classes.

Because they're full of violence and mature content. As with most literary formats, there are some books that are appropriate for all readers and some that require adult supervision. While some graphic novels may contain mature content, so do many award-winning prose novels, such as *Julie of the Wolves*, *Lord of the Flies*, *Of Mice and Men*, and *The Hunger Games*. It is always advisable for parents and teachers to look through books before selecting or assigning them. And if there is no opportunity to read them first, it is advisable to ask knowledgeable colleagues, librarians, or booksellers about intended reading selections.

In an effort to help you find and determine the appropriateness of select graphic novels, we introduce, suggest, and discuss a large selection of our favorite graphic novels throughout this book. We also indicate age and grade appropriateness and whether they contain any mature content that might need vetting. In the Bonus Resource, an online companion download, we provide you with an extensive list of over 200 graphic novels currently available, along with summaries, notes, and grade levels for these books. In Appendix A we provide resources on how to address naysayers and challenges to your reading selections. In Appendix B we offer resources for both creating and using graphic novels in your classroom. Finally, we recommend you check our website periodically, where we will be continually monitoring new works and updating information, and also that you ask your favorite bookseller, librarian, and/or colleagues for guidance when you have questions.

Because their stories are about superheroes and my kids don't really like that kind of stuff. While some graphic novels tell superhero stories, most don't. Graphic novels embrace a wide variety of genres. These genres include realistic fiction, such as *Smile* by Raina Telgemeier; historical fiction, like the *Nathan Hale's Hazardous Tales* series and *Boxers and Saints* by Gene Luen Yang; nonfiction, such as *The Gettysburg Address: A Graphic Adaptation* and *The United States Constitution: A Graphic Adaptation*, both by Jonathan Hennessey; and books about science, such as the *Last of the Sandwalkers* by Jay Hosler and *HowToons* by Dr. Saul Griffith, Nick Dragotta, Ingrid Dragotta, Arwen Griffith, Joost Bonsen, Jeff Parker, Warren Simons, Sandy Jarrel, Meredith McClaren, Jason Marzloff, Leigh B. Estabrooks, Lee Loughridge, Rich Starkings, Comicraft, Jimmy Betancourt, and Andrea Dunlap. Throughout this book you will see examples and sample lesson ideas based on graphic novels, and we encourage you to note the diversity of texts, stories, and genres.

Because I'm afraid I won't meet Common Core or other state standards if my students read graphic novels during our precious class time instead of complex prose. Graphic novels are wonderful tools teachers can use to meet educational standards. Briefly, graphic novels are complex authentic texts that promote both verbal and visual literacies. They contain a rich vocabulary and extensive and concrete use of literary devices. *For weak language learners*, graphic novels' concise text paired with detailed images helps readers decode and comprehend the text, and their format makes reading feel less daunting and more engaging as the concise verbiage highlights effective language usage and vocabulary. *For skilled readers*, graphic novels offer a differently formatted reading experience, using both strategically selected words and images to tell a story, and thereby modeling concise language and aiding in vocabulary acquisition. Graphic novels have also been found to foster and strengthen a variety of learning skills essential for success in and out of the classroom, and are being successfully used to help readers and writers better understand sequence and its effect on storytelling.

Note that we unpack Common Core State Standards (CCSS) in the "Facts" section below, explicitly detailing how graphic novels can help you teach the discrete standards listed.

Fear #3: I Don't Understand What a Graphic Novel Is, So I Don't Know How to Teach It

In regard to the first part of this fear, for practical purposes we can define graphic novels as bound texts composed in comic format – where the story is told through both text and image – in sequentially presented panels that follow guidelines similar if not identical to those followed in classic novels or informational texts.

When it comes to the second part of this fear, how one teaches graphic novels is one of the greatest obstacles teachers feel when contemplating adding these works to their curricula. Showing how to teach a graphic novel is the purpose of this book, and it is directly addressed in the chapters to follow.

Facts

Graphic Novels and Common Core Standards

While the Common Core State Standards have had widespread effects on many of our classrooms, we recognize many of you may no longer use them. In an effort to reach as wide and diverse an audience as possible, we limit our discussion of Common Core Standards to this section and do not list how each of our lessons addresses these standards specifically. Also note that we discuss the anchor standards for reading and writing and not the specific standards grade by grade. Please feel free, however, to contact us with questions you may have, via our websites: meryljaffe.com and taliahurwich.com.

Common Core Anchor Standards for Reading attempt to define what students should be able to read at the end of each grade and correspond to the College and Career Readiness (CCR) anchor standards for reading readiness. These standards include the following:

- Key Ideas and Details (CCSS.ELA-Literacy.CCRA.R.1-3), where students can competently

  - read and understand a text;

  - make logical inferences from it;

  - cite textual evidence (when writing or speaking about the text) to support such inferences;

  - determine central themes of a text and summarize the key supporting details and ideas; and

  - analyze how and why individuals, events, or ideas develop and interact over the course of the text.

- Craft and Structure (CCSS.ELA-Literacy.CCRA.R.4-6), where students can competently

  - interpret words and phrases as used in a text (including technical, connotative, and figurative meanings) and analyze how specific word choices shape meaning or tone;

  - analyze the structure of specific sentences, paragraphs, and/or larger chunks of text to better understand how they relate to each other and the whole; and

  - assess how the author's point of view or purpose shapes the content and style of a text.

- Integration of Knowledge and Ideas (CCSS.ELA-Literacy.CCRA.R.7-9), where students can competently

  - integrate and evaluate content presented in diverse media formats containing visual images, quantitative expressions, and/or verbal text;

  - delineate and evaluate reasoning, relevance, and evidence presented in arguments and/ or claims in a given text; and

  - analyze how two or more texts address similar themes or topics in order to build knowledge or to compare the approaches the authors take.

- Range of Reading and Level of Text Complexity (CCSS.ELA-Literacy.CCRA.R.10), where students can read and comprehend complex literary and informational texts independently and proficiently.

Graphic novels' stories are told through paired text and images, and this often makes it easier for students to more readily recognize and understand developing themes, analyze social interactions, and recognize and incorporate "key ideas and details" (CCSS.ELA-Literacy.CCRA.R.1-3). An uncle of ours loves telling a story of how he was the only student in his class who got 100% on an *Ivanhoe* test because he was the only one who could describe Ivanhoe's shield and coat of arms. He could do this because he was the only one who had read the graphic novel adaptation of the classic, in which the shield and coat of arms were frequently and prominently displayed.

Graphic novels are great tools for teaching "craft and structure of text" (CCSS.ELA-Literacy. CCRA.R.4-6). As you'll see in Chapters 3 and 4, graphic novel stories are told in any number of boxes (of various sizes and shapes), where text and image vie for valuable space, and therefore *everything* represented on the page is intentionally chosen. The critical reading of graphic novels requires readers to evaluate the author's choice of words, sentence structure, images, font size, shape and color, even design for intent and meaning – all of which is required in this standard. In Chapters 4, 5, and 6 we demonstrate how to help students evaluate these choices, thus addressing craft and structure issues that work not only for graphic novels but translate well for analyzing any given text.

Regarding the Common Core Standard "integration of knowledge and ideas" (CCSS.ELA-Literacy.CCRA.R.7-9), graphic novels by their very nature require readers to integrate and evaluate content presented in diverse media formats. And while they have a textual component, they're not limited to text. Instead, they engage in visual and verbal communications, requiring students to engage and discuss multiple ways to communicate and discuss ideas.

Finally, regarding the last anchor standard for reading, "range of reading and level of text complexity" (CCSS.ELA-Literacy.CCRA.R.10), graphic novels offer quite a range of reading and level of text complexity. As we detail in Chapter 6, graphic novels offer both complex vocabulary and sentence structure. Furthermore, they often offer varied types and formats of text.

Figure 1.1 (taken from *Zita the Spacegirl*) displays just one example of the complex vocabulary and sentence structure that graphic novels offer their readers. On these pages, we see Zita talking with Piper. She's rifling through descriptions – alien mug shots – in "Gilliam's Guide to Sentient Species," in the hope of finding who ran off with her friend Joseph in this alien world. In this graphic novel (for ages 8 to 12), the language is both complex and varied, as there are two

FIGURE 1.1 Complex vocabulary and sentence structure in *Zita the Spacegirl*
Source: Ben Hatke, *Zita the Spacegirl* (New York: First Second, 2011), pp. 56–57.

very different types of texts here. The mug shots Zita is looking through contain informational text and images about various alien species, while the graphic novel story continues around this with narrative text and dialogue. On page 56, we read through descriptions of Dozers, Whiskersmiths, and Tentacled Tubbs, after which Zita excitedly shouts, ". . . found him!" On page 57, we see that Zita has identified a Screed, whose species is ". . . dangerous, agile and enigmatic . . . working as bounty hunters and mercenaries." Piper informs Zita, "your friend is in terrible danger," as the tension increases and the hunt begins. As you can see in this example, the vocabulary, language use, sentence complexity, and text formats vary and provide very different reading experiences for readers to navigate (and enjoy).

Common Core Anchor Standards for Writing attempt to define what students should be able to do at the end of each grade, and correspond to the College and Career Readiness (CCR) anchor standards for writing. These standards include the following:

- Text Types and Purposes (CCSS.ELA-Literacy.CCRA.W.1-3), where students can competently

    - write arguments to support claims using valid reasoning and relevant and sufficient evidence;

- write informative/explanatory texts to examine and convey complex ideas and information clearly and accurately through the effective selection, organization, and analysis of content; and

- write narratives that relay real or imagined experiences or events that contain well-chosen details and well-structured event sequences.

- Production and Distribution of Writing (CCSS.ELA-Literacy.CCRA.W.4-6), where students can competently

  - produce clear and coherent writing in which the development, organization, and style are appropriate to the text's task, purpose, and audience;

  - develop and strengthen writing as needed by planning, revising, editing, rewriting, or trying a new approach; and

  - use technology, including the Internet, to produce and publish writing and to interact and collaborate with others.

- Research to Build and Present Knowledge (CCSS.ELA-Literacy.CCRA.W.7-9), where students can competently

  - conduct short and/or more sustained research projects based on focused questions, demonstrating understanding of the subject under investigation;

  - gather relevant information from multiple print and digital sources, assess the credibility and accuracy of each source, and integrate the information while avoiding plagiarism; and

  - draw evidence from literary or informational texts to support analysis, reflection, and research.

- Range of Writing (CCSS.ELA-Literacy.CCRA.W.10), where students can competently write routinely over extended time frames (where time is spent on research, reflection, and revision) and shorter time frames (a single sitting or a day or two) for a range of tasks, purposes, and audiences.

Graphic novels are well suited for teaching and reinforcing "text types and purposes" (CCSS. ELA-Literacy.CCRA.W.1-3). In Chapter 7 we discuss how graphic novels can be used to teach and develop students' expository, creative, and nonfiction writing. They can be particularly beneficial when helping students work on developing well-structured sequences of events (due to their sequentially presented panels), and for determining the use and placement of well-chosen details (due to the limited nature of the choices that need to be made, as mentioned earlier and discussed in greater detail in Chapters 3 and 4).

Graphic novels can be very effective tools for the "production and distribution of writing" (CCSS.ELA-Literacy.CCRA.W.4-6) as well, as addressed in Chapter 7. In particular we detail how graphic novels can help students with planning, collaborating, and editing, and we provide links and online resources for students to produce and publish their own fiction and/or nonfiction graphic novels.

Regarding "research to build and present knowledge" (CCSS.ELA-Literacy.CCRA.W.7-9) and "range of writing" (CCSS.ELA-Literacy.CCRA.W.10), offering students alternate writing formats and assignments often makes the writing experience less daunting. In Chapter 7 we detail how graphic novels can be used for various formats of nonfiction writing, and in Chapter 8 we provide examples of nonfiction and historical fiction graphic novels for classroom use when studying topics in math, science, and social studies. Offering students a greater number of writing options and formats also provides them with greater writing opportunities across wider ranges of tasks, purposes, and audiences.

How and Where to Find Graphic Novels

There are several ways you can find quality graphic novels. We recommend, first, asking your favorite librarian or children's bookseller. You can also find reviews of graphic novels in *Kirkus Reviews*, the *Horn Book Magazine*, and the *Horn Book Guide*, all of which are available in both print and digital form. And (as noted earlier) we provide you with an extensive list of quality kids' graphic novels, along with summaries, special notes, and suggested grade level appropriateness, in our Bonus Resource.

In addition to these lists, here are some other links and resources you'll find valuable:

- Our website will continue to review graphic novels while providing you with lesson suggestions, paired reading suggestions, and additional resource links. Check it out regularly.

- The Association for Library Service to Children (ALSC) has a fairly active link with updated graphic novel reading lists for grades K–2, 3–5, and 6–8. Here is the latest list (compiled in 2016): www.ala.org/alsc/publications-resources/book-lists/graphicnovels2016.

- The Quicklists Consulting Committee of the ALSC has created a list of core titles for starting or maintaining a children's graphic novel collection. This list is updated at least annually and can be found at www.ala.org/alsc/publications-resources/book-lists/graphicnovels2016.

- The *School Library Journal*'s *Good Comics for Kids* is a collaborative blog covering kids' comics written by a group of librarians, parents, and other writers for readers up to age 16. Find it at blogs.slj.com/goodcomicsforkids.

- Meryl and Talia host an ongoing column, "Using Graphic Novels in Education," for the Comic Book Legal Defense Fund (CBLDF). Each column highlights a specific graphic novel, providing a summary, suggested lesson plans, and additional resources, at cbldf.org /?s=using+graphic+novels+in+education.

- Teachers often review graphic novels; here are three blogs we've visited for such reviews:

  - www.goodreads.com/list/show/5038.Best_Graphic_Novels_for_Children;

  - thecomicbookteacher.com; and

  - theothercomicbookteacher.com.

Moving Forward: Using this Book to Help You Read and Integrate Graphic Novels into Your Curricula

In the pages to follow we introduce some our favorite kids' graphic novels to you while detailing how to read them, how to teach reading them, and how to integrate them into your language arts and content-area curricula. Here is an outline of the remaining chapters:

- **Chapter 2, "Why Use Graphic Novels? Why Now?"** shares much of the research that is coming out about graphic novels. We open with this to give you a framework to advocate for their use and also to get a more complete picture of how they might be used in your school and in your classroom.

- **Chapter 3, "Foundational Skills in Graphic Novels, Part 1: Reading Pictures,"** introduces how to read graphic novels by exploring visual literacy and what one must keep in mind when critically reading images. Whether analyzing an advertisement, viewing a newspaper or online photograph, or reading a graphic novel, one must understand not only the author's or artist's intent in the image's construction but also the reasons behind choices made (and not made) in its perspective and design. This chapter is intended to help you teach various visual media formats, including advertisements, photographs, films, and graphic novels.

- **Chapter 4, "Foundational Skills in Graphic Novels, Part 2: How to Teach Graphic Novels,"** focuses more specifically on how to teach your students to critically read graphic novels. We describe how to "read" and teach graphic novels' "anatomy" and essential component elements, while we also provide lesson suggestions and strategies to help you best build your students' graphic novel toolbox and in turn their reading and reading comprehension of graphic novels. We end this chapter by modeling how to critically read a page from one of our favorite graphic novels.

- **Chapter 5, "Motivation,"** critically looks at the motivating nature of graphic novels. It lists several ways graphic novels motivate students, several challenges you may encounter, and strategies to address these challenges in your classroom.

- **Chapter 6, "Using Graphic Novels to Teach Reading,"** opens by discussing challenges you may initially find when using graphic novels for language arts instruction and how best to address those challenges, including the best ways to find and select appropriate graphic novels for your language arts or reading classes, and also ways to get your students to slow down and really "read" the images. We then provide lesson suggestions for using graphic novels as primary or anchor texts for teaching phonics; wordplay, language usage, and vocabulary; reading comprehension and close reading; literary devices; and character development.

- **Chapter 7, "Graphic Novels and the Writing Process,"** explores different ways in which graphic novels are effective tools in the writing classroom. We open with an exploration of how graphic novels can help you highlight and practice skills required not only in graphic novels but in prose fiction writing as well. We then continue with prose nonfiction, exploring different genres of nonfiction, and how graphic novels can develop skills useful in the creation of such written pieces. Finally, we close with details and pointers for teaching the prewriting, writing, and editing processes for comic strips and graphic novels.

- **Chapter 8, "Graphic Novels and Content-Area Curriculum,"** explores various ways graphic novels can be and have been used in content-area classrooms for math, social studies, and science. We provide arguments for their inclusion in these classrooms, suggested reading options, and detailed lesson suggestions.

We hope that with these objectives in mind you enjoy this journey as we discuss and model how and why to use graphic novels for creative and exciting classroom curricula.

WHY USE GRAPHIC NOVELS? WHY NOW?

I am definitely a proponent of graphic novels. My students love them. Isn't the point to foster a love of reading? I want them to become lifelong readers. Sometimes graphic novels are the gateway. Have you seen the vocabulary in some of those novels? It is pretty high. There are some high quality graphic novels out there: *American Born Chinese*, *El Deafo*, *Macbeth*, *Locke and Key*, and many more.

Rachel Lantz, Racine, WI (English Teacher, 6–12)

Graphic Novels Improve and Enhance Teaching Methods

Graphic novels' bursting images and dynamic text invite us to explore diverse worlds, diverse times, and diverse characters. We can't help but feel the horrors and tensions of the civil rights movement of the 1960s; be swept up into sordid revolutions; or ogle at the wonders of fantastical worlds across the globe, in space, or in alternate universes. Readers can experience the humor and horrors of school as seen through the eyes of a spunky mouse, or of typical and not-so-typical teens and tweens much like themselves. Our students read and see metaphors, they read and see hyperbole and onomatopoeia. Furthermore, the texts' fonts are as exciting and inviting as their images. The inclusion of these texts in our classrooms invites *all* kinds of learners (be they avid readers or reluctant readers; be they native English speakers or second language learners) from all types of cultures to be a part of these unfolding stories. Being more inclusive to larger audiences of diverse learners, graphic novels make learning more meaningful.

While parents and teachers are beginning to recognize the engaging and motivational aspects of graphic novels, their integration into home and school libraries, especially for K–8 students, has been slow at best. This is, in part, because many of these parents and educators are not comfortable reading the medium, they don't always know how or where to find these great reading options, and there's been little research documenting these texts' use and effect in elementary and middle school classrooms. To date, word of their successful integration in K–8 settings is primarily passed down anecdotally or in teachers' magazines and journals. Empirical studies are still rare. As Aşkın H. Yıldırım (2013) comments:

> The use of graphic novels in language classrooms has a short history, and therefore its literature is rather limited. Although there are not many comprehensive studies assessing their impact as teaching tools, the feedback from educators and scholars as to the use of graphic novels in language classrooms is a clear indication of their worth as a pedagogical tool. Many experts in the field suggest that they can be used in classrooms with many different purposes. (p. 119)

From the research that is available, studies are beginning to show particular effects.

- Visual educational content aids memory and comprehension while making content more meaningful and accessible.

- Graphic novels and other multimodal classroom content make abstract concepts more concrete, aid in teaching language usage and sequencing, and more clearly address twenty-first century communication in our communities and workplaces. Moreover, graphic novels are uniquely designed multimodal texts whose benefits are equally unique.

- Graphic novels motivate all kinds of readers and learners and have been found to engage students – increasing the number of books they read, words they encounter, and worlds they explore.

In this chapter, we present snapshots of what researchers are finding about the effects of using graphic novels in lower and middle school classrooms. We organize the research along the previously mentioned points. Knowing this body of research, we believe, will enable you to address latent concerns others may still have about your using graphic novels. Moreover, recognizing what graphic novels have been proven to do can empower their successful integration into your classrooms and libraries!

We start by addressing the power of graphic novels' visual content.

The Power of Visual Educational Content to Boost Academic Performance

In terms of the effect of visual content on academic performance, a good deal of research is showing how illustrations and visualization aid memory and comprehension. Studies in perception indicate that people process visual content much faster than they process verbal content. In "Visual Literacy: What You Get Is What You See," Lynell Burmark (2008) cites the finding that "humans process visuals an astounding 60,000 times faster than text" (p. 7). Scott McCloud (1993) notes that "pictures are **received** information. We need no formal education to 'get the message.' The message is *instantaneous*. Writing is **perceived** information. It takes time and specialized knowledge to decode the abstract symbols of language" (p. 49; emphasis added).

Karen Feathers and Poonam Arya (2015) recently examined how young readers (third graders) use visual information during reading (p. 42). Students were asked to read an illustrated text and retell it. The researchers examined students' strategic use of text and image for reading comprehension. While these researchers used illustrated texts and not graphic novels, their findings are important in that they support students' use of image for comprehension. More specifically, these authors report that "while children sometimes looked at images to support word recognition, they used images to a greater extent to construct meaning. . . . This deliberate use of images suggests that children viewed [them] as semiotic space" (pp. 57–59).

The power of images to relay content and information is not new. What is much more recent is our considering the art and skill of "reading" images as a form of literacy indispensable in the Information Age. Looking specifically at the importance of teaching visual literacy, Sylvia Pantaleo (2014) examined sixth- through eighth-grade students' comfort when reading images, and its effect on their academic performance. To do so, she worked with a teacher, "Mrs. K," and her language arts students. They taught students about the visual elements of art and design in graphic novels and picture books through guided lessons, interviews, and written and visual work as well as observations and reflections. Pantaleo demonstrates that teaching visual literacy (i.e. an understanding of visual perspectives as well as the physical aspects of text and image design) improves students' ability to make meaning of their culture and their world (p. 48). Additionally, E. Sutton Flynt and William Brozo (2010) report that teaching visual literacy across the curriculum can lead to improvement in verbal skills; self-expression and ordering of ideas; and student motivation, self-image and self-reliance, independence, and confidence (p. 528).

The Power of Paired Visual and Verbal Educational Content and Multimodal Literacies to Boost Academic Performance

While the term *visual literacy* is credited to John Debes in 1969, it was the scholars of the New London Group[*] who opened the concept up to a much broader discussion and audience in 1996. The New London Group (1996) argued that "literacy pedagogy has traditionally meant teaching and learning to read and write in page-bound, official, standard forms of the national language" (pp. 60–61). To better assure academic and social success in contemporary classrooms, the members of the New London Group call for a reorientation of literacy education – a "multiliteracies" approach.

While posited in the 1990s, the need for multiple literacies is even more evident in the twenty-first century, where we communicate on Facebook, YouTube, Pinterest, Snapchat, and Twitter; use abbreviated text and emoji while playing smartphone games or using apps; and so much more. In discussing the multiple literacies commonly used in workspaces and communities and in our public lives, the New London Group states:

> Increasingly important are modes of meaning other than Linguistic, including Visual Meanings (images, page layouts, screen formats); Audio Meanings (music, sound effects); Gestural Meanings (body language, sensuality); Spatial Meanings (the meanings of environmental spaces, architectural spaces); and Multimodal Meaning. (p. 83)

What makes graphic novels particularly appealing when discussing classroom use and multiple literacies is the degree to which text, images, font styles, and panel designs all work collaboratively and cumulatively to construct the story. This is, in fact, a type of literacy the New London Group calls "multimodal" literacy. They argue that "of the modes of meaning, the Multimodal is

[*]The New London Group comprised the following scholars: Courtney Cazden, Bill Cope, James Cook, Norman Fairclough, Jim Gee, Mary Kalantzis, Gunther Kress, Allan Luke, Carmen Luke, Sara Michaels, and Martin Nakata.

the most significant, as it relates all the other modes in quite remarkably dynamic relationships" (p. 80). Furthermore, McCloud (1993) writes:

> Pictures can induce strong feelings in the reader, but they can also lack the specificity of words. Words, on the other hand, offer that specificity, but can lack the immediate emotional charge of pictures, relying instead on a gradual **cumulative** effect. **Together**, of course, words and pictures can make miracles. (p. 135)

In addition to their multimodal components, graphic novels have another unique aspect that positions them well for classroom use: their interaction with space, image, and time. In this way, graphic novels are more successful than other visual and spatial mediums, such as animation and film. Gene Yang (2008), an author and educator, notes that while "language and actions in film and animation are time-bound," information and the concept of time progress "only as quickly as your eyes move across the page" (p. 188). With graphic novels, students can view and review material at their own pace. Films, in contrast, are shared visual experiences that are much more difficult for students to absorb independently.

In the sections that follow, we introduce you to research that has illuminated the ways that multimodal literacy (specifically in graphic novels) engages students and aids them in the classroom.

Graphic novels' multimodal content boosts vocabulary and language use

In studies examining youth literacy, researchers have found that graphic novels boost students' vocabulary. Sylvia Pantaleo (2011) has documented how graphic novels build vocabulary. In another study, Stephen Krashen (2004) found that comics and graphic novels offer 20% more rare vocabulary than traditional chapter books and that by reading a comic book every day, young readers process about 500,000 words a year, of which most are "complex vocabulary with a respectable level of difficulty" (p. 98). Supporting Krashen's research, librarians and teachers are noting on blogs and in newspapers and magazines that graphic novels not only boost the amount of time kids spend reading and building complex vocabulary but are also excellent tools for teaching literary devices.

Investigating the use of literary devices in graphic novels, Ashley Dallacqua (2012) examined fifth-grade students in a suburban parochial school in a Midwestern city. Through book discussions and student interviews, Dallacqua found that not only were students able to recognize verbal and visual uses of symbolism, metaphor, allusion, point of view, and other literary devices throughout the various graphic novels they read, but they were also able to more efficiently recognize and understand them in prose novels read subsequently. Dallacqua notes, "All of [the literary] concepts [in the prose novel *The Giver*] came alive for my students by recalling concepts and images from [the graphic novel] *The Arrival*" (p. 375). Ultimately, Dallacqua concludes, "Graphic novels, like the ones used in this study, stand equally with print-based literature as complex, academically challenging, and rich with literary elements and devices" (p. 376).

While studying the use of graphic novels for developing fourth graders' comprehension strategies (discussed in greater detail later), Beverley Brenna (2013) found that after studying a number of age-appropriate graphic novels, "literary techniques discussed by these Grade 4 students included an identification of onomatopoeia as a common inclusion in the textual 'sound track' of graphic novels, as well as other literary techniques" (p. 92). Sally Brown (2013) notes that when reading and discussing graphic novels with second graders, "The expression in their voices illustrates a true understanding of the ways in which onomatopoeia adds richness to a story" (p. 211). Furthermore, Brown posits that "the nature of the dialog, multiple characters, onomatopoeia, rapidly changing punctuation, and short amounts of text provided opportunities to practice fluency" (p. 212).

Looking more specifically at graphic novels' use of literary devices, Rachel Williams (2008) studied 146 sixth-grade English language arts and reading students in West Texas. Williams investigated whether the use of graphic novels and comic book character instruction would affect students' comprehension of figurative language, specifically, their comprehension of similes, metaphors, idioms, hyperbole, and personification. A treatment and a control group were used, and significant differences were found. Williams concludes that graphic novel instruction could be used to improve the comprehension of figurative language in general and of idioms in particular.

Graphic novels' multimodal content boosts sequencing skills

Graphic novels' stories are told in boxes or panels that are arranged in sequences (typically from left to right) across the page, and the art of navigating and following these discrete panels must be learned. Whether reading or writing graphic novels, students *must* slow down and pay attention to the panel details and to panel sequence.

There has been some scholarly research investigating how cartoons and graphic novels have been used to help early readers understand sequencing. By the very nature of their use of sequential art in storytelling, graphic novels lend themselves as tools for teaching and more clearly understanding sequencing. Jesse Karp (2011), an early childhood and interdivisional librarian, notes that graphic novels are great tools to reinforce the left-to-right sequence needed for reading. She notes that not only is the written text sequenced from left to right (as in any other text), but the panels and images are similarly sequenced from left to right.

Maggie Chase, Eun Hye Son, and Stan Steiner (2014) have detailed one such example from their examination of students' understanding of story sequence. After familiarizing students with graphic novels, they selected comic strips from graphic novels, cut them up into individual panels, and had students arrange them into a chronological order that made sense to them. Once this was mastered, students were asked to tell their stories and then write them. These educators found that all their students' writing demonstrated a clear understanding of sequencing in storytelling.

Graphic novels' multimodal content boosts comprehension and critical thinking

Research is only starting to demonstrate how the dynamic relationship between words and images found in graphic novels engages students' creativity, comprehension, and analytic skills. This point seems to hold true both in practice and in theory. To comprehend stories told in graphic novels, readers must actively construct the story, integrating text and image while pausing and then jumping from panel to panel. Not only must readers integrate the given text, image, and panel design, they must also construct, synthesize, and comprehend what isn't given. Scott McCloud (1993) notes that "this phenomenon of observing the parts but perceiving the whole" (p. 63) is called "closure." He further notes that when readers encounter closure, they effectively "mentally complet[e] that which is incomplete." In a similar vein, Buffy Edwards (2009) reflects that reading a graphic novel requires the reader to infer and construct meaning from the visual representations while using the text not only to develop meaning but to foster comprehension (pp. 56–58).

Research is beginning to illustrate how the pairing of image and text practically shape – and at times improve – students' comprehension skills. Claudia McVicker (2007) found that teaching with graphic novels aids learning and reading comprehension (pp. 85–88). In another study, Jason Ranker (2007) found that teaching with graphic novels aids in distinguishing textual differences between narrative and dialogue (p. 304). Daniela Elsner (2013) notes that research has shown that "weak readers are very often not able to mentally visualize text chunks or passages, which is one of the prime prerequisites for successful comprehension" (p. 56). As a result, it is perhaps not surprising that when she interviewed students about their reading graphic novels in their English lessons, asking why they particularly enjoyed graphic novels, "the students answered that the graphic novels were easier to understand and that the pictures had their part in this" (p. 67). Furthermore, it's been demonstrated that people learn more deeply and effectively, and recall more efficiently, from illustrated texts than from text alone (Levie & Lentz, 1982). These factors compel us as educators to seriously consider the use of graphic novels as invaluable educational tools.

While research focusing on graphic novels' cognitive benefits for students in the lower and middle school grades is limited, three studies stand out and deserve mention.

Examining fifth-grade students, Kimberly Jennings, Audrey Rule, and Sarah Vander Zanden (2014) compare graphic novels not only with prose novels but with heavily illustrated novels, such as *The Strange Adventures of Hugo Cabret* and *Diary of Wimpy Kid*. During the 2011 to 2012 academic year, 24 mixed-ability fifth graders selected two traditional novels, two heavily illustrated novels, and two graphic novels from a suggested reading list. They participated in literature circles and discussion groups structured with thinking skills, and completed reading, writing, and creative assignments after reading the books. Student comprehension and enjoyment were measured after reading and completing assignments for each book selected. Jennings, Rule, and Zanden found that student responses to assessment prompts after reading heavily illustrated prose and prose novels were significantly less detailed than their responses to graphic novels. Interestingly, there was no significant difference between student responses to heavily illustrated texts versus prose texts. These results suggest that the multimodality of graphic novels and not simply the visual representations are educationally valuable and worth further study. Heavily illustrated novels use literary modes as well as visual modes of communication, but the images and text function parallel to each other – never intersecting. Conversely, graphic novels are unique because their text, images, and design complement, intersect, and build concrete and inferential materials together.

Beverley Brenna (2013), in a different study, worked with fourth graders to determine what comprehension strategies students might learn to apply when studying age-appropriate graphic novels, and in what ways these graphic novels might support their development as readers. Brenna observed the students and worked with them in small groups, supporting comprehension strategies introduced to the whole class by the classroom teacher as they studied three graphic novels (*Binky the Space Cat* by Ashley Spires, *Babymouse: Queen of the World* by Jennifer Holm and Matthew Holm, and a graphic novel adaptation of *The Tale of Despereaux* by Matt Smith and David Tilton). Among her findings, she noted that some of the students' comments dealt with mature and complex topics, such as narrative distance. From such a finding, she reflected, "That such a discussion could occur at this grade level is a tribute to the students' deep involvement in the reading and the richness offered within the graphic texts at hand" (p. 92). Brenna concluded:

> [I]t is anticipated that these strategies could consciously be applied to the reading of visual images outside the classroom. . . . [S]ome of the particular cues . . . such as narrative distance, have the potential to be applied in other more abstract contexts, and may prove helpful to developing writers as well as developing readers in terms of executive functioning related to the reading and writing process. (p. 92)

Finally, Sally Brown's (2013) research is notable not only for her meeting with second-grade students, but for the diversity found in her group, which was "approximately 59% African American, 32% Latino, and 9% European American." Seven of the students were English learners whose first language was Spanish. Thirteen of the students in her study were considered to be reading below grade level. She had students first read *Babymouse: Queen of the World* (by Jennifer Holm and Matthew Holm) and conducted small group discussions based on the language arts teacher's whole class lessons. She found that

> [t]hrough the initial immersion in graphic novels, the students' understanding of story was enhanced as they internalized characters, their emotions, and actions by reading in a series of graphic novels. . . . Through minilessons, students were encouraged to observe the ways in which the authors developed plot in various settings using the same characters. All of these experiences served as a scaffold for comprehension of the stories. (p. 215)

In short, Brown found in her study, "The short text plus images provided access to interesting characters and complex plots. Visual and written modes were necessary for comprehension" (p. 215).

Graphic novels' multimodal content boosts memory

While there is no direct quantitative research to date analyzing how graphic novels aid memory, it is believed that because our brains must process verbal and visual information as we decode and read graphic novels, this creates additional memory associations and pathways. As a result, we are storing similar information across different pathways and areas of our brain, making data retrieval that much more efficient. Katalin Orbán (2013) proposes that graphic novels are a particularly good match to the subject of memory because they rely on multisensory processing. She explains that "as the neuroscience of memory is beginning to find, differences in the storing and accessibility of particular memories are often linked to the differences and complex interplay of sensory stimuli, due to the existence of two interconnected memory systems" (p. 4).

Graphic Novels Motivate All Kinds of Readers and Learners

It is being increasingly noted by teachers that graphic novels' vibrant images, playful fonts, and inviting dialogues make reading these complex texts more fun and accessible for all kinds of readers and learners. We have previously spoken about how the vibrant and inviting nature of graphic novels have led to deeper analyses, but we now want to highlight a more fundamental strength of graphic novels: graphic novels have been shown time and time again to increase student motivation. Indeed, citing research dating back to the 1940s, Gene Yang (2003) notes, "By far, the most frequently mentioned asset of comics as an educational tool is its ability to motivate students" (n.p.).

This history of research connecting graphic novels to increased motivation continues to this day. Studies such as Stephen Krashen's *The Power of Reading* (2004) show that when students choose their own reading materials, they are more passionate about what they read and, perhaps unsurprisingly, show improvement in their reading skills. Jesse Karp (2011) further says: "It will come as little surprise to anyone who works with children and young adults that graphic novels disappear from library shelves faster than anything else and are the topic of eager discussion whenever they find their way into classrooms" (p. 34). Finally, looking specifically at middle school reading choices, Karen Gavigan (2014) conducted a multiple case study of six middle school library circulation records during the 2011–2012 academic year. She found that graphic novel titles are extremely high circulators in both school and public libraries (p. 103). She also found equal numbers of avid versus struggling readers using graphic novels in four of the six libraries, but no classroom teachers were taking these books out. It was the students themselves selecting these books. Jennings, Rule, and Zanden (2014) found that graphic novels were rated significantly more enjoyable and understandable than prose and heavily illustrated novels. Their study found that "students reported greatest enjoyment in reading, most interest for the story and greatest understanding of graphic novels followed by heavily-illustrated novels and then traditional novels" (p. 266).

Not only do graphic novels pique students' interest, motivating them to read, but studies have also shown that many students reading graphic novels are motivated to read prose texts as well. Joanne Ujiie and Stephen Krashen (1996), surveying students from several socioeconomic backgrounds, examined their reading patterns. They found that "for both groups, those who read more comic books did more pleasure reading, liked to read more, and tended to read more books" (p. 54). This suggests that graphic novels can be tools for empowering teachers and readers as well as motivating them.

Researchers have found a few other ways that graphic novels empower students by making lessons more relevant, varied, and interesting. Donna Alverman and Shelley Xu (2003) claim that "because popular culture texts are part of students' everyday literacies, they hold powerful and personal meanings for students" (p. 150). Joy Lawn (2012), considering reluctant readers, notes that graphic novels "remove any stigma attached to reading difficulties" (p. 31). Moreover, "They look interesting and, often, edgy. They don't look like books for very young readers; they don't make struggling readers look unintelligent" (p. 31).

Finally, research has shown that reading graphic novels can motivate students in their written assignments as well. After studying graphic novels and having second-grade students write their own graphic stories, Brown (2013) said:

> Before this project, the students mainly wrote in journals based on teacher prompts. Overall, the class wrote simple stories consisting of a few sentences and complained about writing. . . . [After the class studied graphic novels, all of their] graphic stories contained the story elements of characters, setting, and plot, which were not always included in their journal writing. Fourteen of the eighteen stories had sophisticated storylines for this grade level. . . . The project seemed to motivate students as writers. More than half of the class indicated that they now considered writing "fun" and wanted to engage in more projects in which they could use speech bubbles. (p. 216)

Brown also noted that not only did graphic novels seem to excite these second-grade students, they helped build their confidence as readers and writers. Brown noted that their diverse group of second graders were all actively engaged in learning and that graphic novels "provided accessibility to critical conversations" (p. 216).

Responding to the Naysayers: The Complex History of Graphic Novels and Why Now Is the Time to Use Them

Considering the research we've shared with you – research showing graphic novels' positive impact on multimodal literacy, vocabulary and language use, sequencing, critical thinking, comprehension, and motivation – we hope you have a sense of how promising a medium graphic novels can be. However, empowerment goes beyond understanding why graphic novels are powerful educational tools. Empowerment involves being able to respond to a long history of naysayers who are skeptical, if not hostile to the idea of including graphic novels in the home and classroom. In the following sections, we take you through comics' sordid history and also discuss why and how things have changed.

Why There Has Been Resistance

One reason we don't see a lot of graphic novels in K–8 curricula is because some educators feel that replacing a portion of the teaching time now devoted to standard prose with time spent on graphic novels will result in a decline in overall literacy. Graphic novels are often associated with comics and the Sunday funny pages – lots of fluff and fun, but definitely not worth valuable classroom time. In this chapter, we have debunked that opinion and shown you how graphic novels help student vocabulary, memory, sequencing, critical thinking, critical reading, and reading comprehension. In the following chapters, we will show you how graphic novels are actually complex texts that not only motivate students but are viable literary works in their own right.

Another source of resistance is that even among those teachers interested in incorporating graphic novels into their lessons, many don't know how to read them comprehensively or how to find the burgeoning cache of quality graphic novels for kids that have recently been published. Both of these issues are addressed throughout this book as we make graphic novel reading suggestions, and demonstrate how to critically read them as well as how to successfully incorporate them into your curriculum.

The sad truth is that most of the resistance to graphic novels in education stems from the misguided (although possibly well-intentioned) work of Dr. Fredric Wertham and his testimony before the 1954 Senate Committee on juvenile delinquency. Wertham, a German-born American psychiatrist, was a champion of human rights and a key speaker instrumental in the *Brown v. Board of Education* Supreme Court desegregation decision. In the midst of our country's concern about increasing crime rates, McCarthyism, and the balance of our moral fiber, Wertham argued that the then-popular comics and pulp fiction directly affected youth and led to juvenile delinquency.

On sabbatical from his clinic work with underprivileged youth in Harlem in New York City, Wertham wrote "What Parents Don't Know About Comic Books." In this article, Wertham (1953/2007) warned, "Chronic stimulation, temptation and seduction by comic books is a contributing factor to many children's maladjustment" (p. 52). The article continued by making a broad case that "normal" children were the ones most harmed by comic books and pop culture. Wertham's book *Seduction of the Innocent*, published a year later in 1954, made an even stronger case for the link between comic books and juvenile delinquency.

As Dave Itzkoff (2013) wrote in the *New York Times*: "Wertham's influence was indisputable." Wertham's publications coincided with a US Senate Committee investigation on the causes and influence of juvenile delinquency. Public pressure (arising from televised and reported committee proceedings) forced comic book producers to draw up a self-imposed Comics Code, to be applied by the Comics Code Authority that was formed by the newly established Comic Magazine Association of America (CMAA). The code restricted sex, violence, curse words, lewd images, and criticism of religion. Comic books were not allowed to be sold on newsstands without the Comics Code Authority seal. As a result, many comic book companies disappeared or became mere shadows of their former selves. In Carol Tilley's (2012) words, "Even though comics publishers also faced increasing competition from the nascent television industry for children's attention, the CMAA's code effectively marked the end of comics' reign as the most popular print medium among children in history" (p. 385).

It has taken decades for comics and graphic novels to recover. At first, comics went underground. They were no longer sold at newspaper stands but in underground comic book stores to avoid censorship. Furthermore, with the advent of *Mad Magazine*, comics turned to satire and covered a wider range of genres and themes. The industry slowly began to grow and recover. In 1971, the Comics Code was eased and altered, and in 2011, the Comics Code Authority became defunct.

Why Things Are Changing Now

A few factors are now helping to usher comics and graphic novels into classrooms and libraries, offering them as a respectable and educationally valuable resource. There have been changes in publishing, changes in markets and marketing, and since the turn of the twenty-first century, there have been cries for change from academics and educators – changes that graphic novels have been particularly qualified to address.

After the success of the graphic novel *Maus* by Art Spiegelman in the 1980s and early 1990s, and its winning the Pulitzer Prize in 1992, publishers began producing sophisticated graphic novels in a variety of genres. These high-quality, high-interest, sophisticated graphic novels began winning prestigious awards. Publishers also began setting up their own children's book imprints, publishing graphic novels specifically for kids. Librarians, noticing the increased traffic and interest in reading, particularly among tweens, teens, and young adults, became strong advocates for graphic novels, introducing them to kids, parents, and educators. Furthermore, shortly after the burst in kids' comic publishing, Wertham's *Seduction of the Innocent* was discredited.

In 2010, when Wertham's papers were made widely available, researchers were able to scrutinize his research. Carol Tilley (2012), an assistant professor in the Graduate School of Library and Information Science at the University of Illinois, found numerous examples in which Wertham manipulated, overstated, compromised, and fabricated evidence. Tilley exposed how he exaggerated the number of youth he interviewed, misstated their ages, combined quotations to make his point, omitted extenuating circumstances in the lives of his patients, and at times invented details. It was shown that on the evidence of only a handful of interviews with disadvantaged youth, Wertham built his case, applying it to all American youth.

In book markets today, graphic novels are the fastest growing categories in publishing and bookselling, and are far more sophisticated, in terms of their art, their language use, and their content, than their comic predecessors. Furthermore, like their counterparts in prose, graphic novels are now being written and published in every conceivable genre: fiction, historical fiction, memoir, biography, history, fantasy, romance, adventure, science fiction, and popular (and not so popular) science. These graphic novels are being reviewed by *Kirkus Reviews*, the *School Library Journal*, the *Horn Book Magazine*, and many other publications. Finally, graphic novels such as *El Deafo*, *This One Summer*, *Nimona*, and *March* are receiving Newbery Honors and Caldecott Honors and are becoming National Book Award finalists.

Graphic novels' burgeoning popularity is also in part due to growing changes in education. On the academic front, for example, the New London Group and others have been emphasizing the need for exploring multiple literacies (visual, verbal, cultural, digital, etc.). The New London Group's call for multiple literacies was soon addressed by the Common Core State Standards Initiative, which is mandating the teaching of complex, authentic, multimodal texts. Here, too, graphic novels squarely meet those demands.

How to Be Part of the Change

In the pages to follow, we will introduce you to many outstanding graphic novels that can and should be used in elementary and middle school classrooms. Assessing your kids' needs, we provide lesson suggestions on how graphic novels can be integrated into your read-alouds, your free reading, and your lessons to meet your diverse student cultures, student skills, and student preferences. We will discuss how you can create dialogues around these books and how to garner support in your school, particularly from the remaining, reluctant graphic-novel naysayers, and provide you with direction and resources for those who may challenge graphic novel suggestions. Finally, in each chapter we will provide you with assessment tools, ways to access lists of quality graphic novels for all ages and levels, and resources and links to take our suggested lessons further.

It's a burgeoning and exciting new world for readers and teachers, and we will gladly usher you in.

REFERENCES

Alverman, D. E., & Xu, S. H. (2003). Children's Everyday Literacies: Intersections of Popular Culture and Language Arts Instruction. *Language Arts*, 81(2), 145–154.

Brenna, B. (2013). How Graphic Novels Support Reading Comprehension Strategy Development in Children. *Literacy*, 47(2), 88–94.

Brown, S. (2013). A Blended Approach to Reading and Writing Graphic Stories. *The Reading Teacher*, 67(3), 208–219.

Burmark, L. (2008). Visual Literacy: What You Get Is What You See. In N. Frey & D. B. Fisher (Eds.), *Teaching Visual Literacy: Using Comic Books, Graphic Novels, Anime, Cartoons, and More to Develop Comprehension and Thinking Skills* (pp. 5–27). Thousand Oaks, CA: Corwin.

Chase, M., Son, E. H., & Steiner, S. (2014). Sequencing and Graphic Novels with Primary-Grade Students. *The Reading Teacher*, 67(6), 435–443. Retrieved from https://doi.org/10.1002/trtr.1242.

Dallacqua, A. K. (2012). Exploring Literary Devices in Graphic Novels. *Language Arts*, 89(6), 365–378.

Edwards, B. (2009). Motivating Middle School Learners: The Graphic Novel Link. *School Library Media Activities Monthly*, 25(8), 56–58.

Elsner, D. (2013). Graphic Novels in the Limelight of a Multiliteracies Approach to Teaching English. In D. Elsner, S. Helff, & B. Viebrock (Eds.), *Films, Graphic Novels & Visuals: Developing Multiliteracies in Foreign Language Education – An Interdisciplinary Approach* (pp. 55–71). Berlin: LIT Verlag.

Feathers, K. M., & Arya, P. (2015). Exploring Young Children's Use of Illustrations in a Picturebook. *Language and Literacy*, 17(1), 42–62.

Flynt, E. S., & Brozo, W. (2010). Visual Literacy and the Content Classroom: A Question of Now, Not When. *The Reading Teacher*, 63(6), 526–528.

Gavigan, K. W. (2014). Shedding New Light on Graphic Novel Collections: A Circulation and Collection Analysis Study in Six Middle School Libraries. *School Libraries Worldwide*, 20(1), 97–115.

Itzkoff, D. (2013, February 19). Scholar Finds Flaws in Work by Archenemy of Comics. *New York Times*. Retrieved from http://www.nytimes.com/2013/02/20/books/flaws-found-in-fredric-werthams-comic-book-studies.html

Jennings, K. A., Rule, A. C., & Vander Zanden, S. M. (2014). Fifth Graders' Enjoyment, Interest, and Comprehension of Graphic Novels Compared to Heavily-Illustrated and Traditional Novels. *International Electronic Journal of Elementary Education*, 6(2), 257–274.

Karp, J. (2011, August). The Power of Words and Pictures: Graphic Novels in Education. *American Libraries*, 42(7/8), 34–35.

Krashen, S. D. (2004). *The Power of Reading: Insights from the Research*. (2nd ed.) Santa Barbara, CA: Libraries Unlimited.

Lawn, J. (2012). Frame by Frame: Understanding the Appeal of the Graphic Novel for the Middle Years. *Learning Literacy: The Middle Years*, 20(1), 26–36.

Levie, W. H., & Lentz, R. (1982). Effects of Text Illustrations: A Review of Research. *Educational Communication and Technology*, 30(4), 195–232.

McCloud, S. (1993). *Understanding Comics: The Invisible Art* (Reprint edition). New York: William Morrow Paperbacks.

McVicker, C. J. (2007). Comic Strips as a Text Structure for Learning to Read. *The Reading Teacher*, 61(1), 85–88. Retrieved from https://doi.org/10.1598/RT.61.1.9.

New London Group. (1996). A Pedagogy of Multiliteracies: Designing Social Futures. *Harvard Educational Review*, 66(1), 60–93.

Orbán, K. (2013). Embodied Reading: The Graphic Novel, Perception, and Memory. International Journal of the Humanities*: Annual Review*, 11.

Pantaleo, S. (2011). Grade 7 Students Reading Graphic Novels: "You Need to Do a Lot of Thinking." *English in Education*, 45(2), 113–131.

Pantaleo, S. (2014). Reading Images in Graphic Novels: Taking Students to a "Greater Thinking Level." *English in Australia*, 49(1), 38–51.

Ranker, J. (2007). Using Comic Books as Read-Alouds: Insights on Reading Instruction from an English as a Second Language Classroom. *The Reading Teacher*, 61(4), 296–305. Retrieved from https://doi.org/10.1598/RT.61.4.2.

Tilley, C. L. (2012). Seducing the Innocent: Fredric Wertham and the Falsifications That Helped Condemn Comics. *Information & Culture*, 47(4), 383–413.

Ujiie, J., & Krashen, S. D. (1996). Comic Book Reading, Reading Enjoyment, and Pleasure Reading Among Middle Class and Chapter I Middle School Students. *Reading Improvement*, 33, 51–54.

Wertham, F. (1954). *Seduction of the Innocent*. London: Museum Press.

Wertham, F. (2007, November 25). Dr. Fredric Wertham's "What Parents Don't Know About Comic Books." (Blog post.) Retrieved from http://learning2share.blogspot.com/2007/11/dr-fredric-werthams-what-parents-dont.html. Originally published in the *Ladies' Home Journal*, November 1953, 51–53, 214–220.

Williams, R. M.-C. (2008). Image, Text, and Story: Comics and Graphic Novels in the Classroom. *Art Education*, 61(6), 13–19.

Yang, G. (2003). *Strengths of Comics in Education*. Retrieved December 2, 2015, from http://www.geneyang.com/comicsedu/strengths.html.

Yang, G. (2008). Graphic Novels in the Classroom. *Language Arts*, 85(3), 185–192.

Yıldırım, A. H. (2013). Using Graphic Novels in the Classroom. *Journal of Language and Literature*, 8, 118–131.

3

FOUNDATIONAL SKILLS IN GRAPHIC NOVELS, PART 1
READING PICTURES

I don't use graphic novels in my class simply because I'm not exactly sure how to yet . . .

I love [them] but am new to using them in my classroom. I need resources to start . . .

I have never used graphic novels but am interested in doing so . . .

The sentiments quoted at the start of this chapter are by far the most frequent reasons teachers attending our panels and workshops give us when asked why they don't use or teach graphic novels in their classrooms. Our goal in this chapter and the next four is to provide you with the tools and language to critically read, teach, and discuss this literary format.

We've broken how to teach graphic novels down into basic components. The first component involves making sure your students can critically read and evaluate images. The second component involves providing students with the vocabulary and logistic skills necessary for critically reading, evaluating, and discussing images in general and the graphic novel format specifically.

In this chapter, we address how to "read" and construct images to relay a persuasive story or argument. Your students must understand how to read images and assess the author's or artist's design choices before they can critically read the books themselves. This is because everything on a graphic novel's page is intentional. The images, the panel and page designs, what's included and what's not included, are all chosen to relay specific details, emotions, and content.

While you're probably very familiar with your students' verbal literacy skills, you may not know what their visual literacy skills are. We therefore recommend that before teaching with graphic novels, you establish baseline visual literacy skills.

Visual Literacy: Teaching How to Critically Read an Image

Visual literacy refers to the ability to critically read, interpret, and persuasively relay content (i.e. a story, an argument, a moment in time, a thought, etc.) through images or visual messages. It is the ability to understand an image's (concrete and inferential) message, its use of symbols, and the rationales for the artist's various compositional choices.

Whether the image one studies is an advertisement, painting, photograph, or graphic novel panel, the way that item is framed, the viewing angle or perspective, the moment in time depicted, and the specific contents (included and omitted), all influence and shape a message. Even the colors and shading relay information as they create contrasts that highlight specific elements, actions, or emotions within the story or message, while allowing others to blend into the background.

Exploring What Visual Literacy Is

To help you understand how visual literacy impacts the reading of graphic novels, we'd like you to temporarily play the role of student in the following exercise. Our intention is to illustrate how complex visual literacy can be, as images often contain considerable detail requiring substantial attention, thought, and analysis.

We'd like you to examine Figure 3.1, a panel from *March: Book One*, by John Lewis, Andrew Ayden, and Nate Powell. (Later, in Chapter 4, after we've presented the tools necessary for reading and discussing graphic novels, we will share what we came up with from examining this figure. As you compare your responses to ours, note that there often is no one "correct" interpretation when close reading graphic [or prose] novels.)

Story Background. *March: Book One* is the first volume of a three-volume memoir by Congressman John Lewis of his life and role in the civil rights movement. While the book opens with the inauguration of President Barack Obama, it then goes back in time to when Lewis was a boy growing up on a small farm in Alabama. In the panel shown here, John Lewis reflects upon how he would read the Bible by himself at age 5, how he'd practice preaching to his "flock" (of chickens), and how one Bible passage particularly struck him.

Figure 3.1 shows the top panel of page 27, and it is one large image with two smaller panels embedded within. We've chosen this panel because the text is as much part of the artistic design as are the illustrations.

As you look at this image, we'd like you to consider the following questions (recording your notes or thoughts elsewhere – we'll return to them a bit later). Feel free to reflect and/or expand upon these questions or to tweak them as seems fit.

- What jumps out at you?

- What surprises you in terms of what is or is not in the image?

- Why is text relayed in different fonts and font sizes?

- What is being communicated in the images and text? What are we expected to infer from the images and text?

FIGURE 3.1 Artistic use of text in *March: Book One*
Source: John Lewis, Andrew Ayden, and Nate Powell, *March: Book One* (Marietta, GA: Top Shelf Productions, 2013), p. 27.

In this and the next chapter, we model and discuss elements and strategies for teaching visual literacy. If you'd like more background or exposure to the world and skills of visual literacy, Scott McCloud's *Understanding Comics* and *Making Comics* are outstanding resources. Both books explore the use of color, fonts, design, shading, perspective, and panel or image composition for those making or reading graphic novels. Furthermore, both books are frequently used by teachers, as anchor texts and as reference texts, when teaching with graphic novels.

Assessing Your Students' Visual Literacy

In the previous section, we highlighted some of the questions skilled readers of graphic novels consider while reading. In this section, we give you the tools necessary to assess how visually literate your students are. More specifically, we help you get a sense of the details your students notice in an image and the types of follow-up questions you may need to ask them.

You can use the following lesson suggestion and rubric to assess your students' visual literacy skills. We suggest assessing their ability to critically read images before you embark on a unit using graphic novels. Note that this assessment activity asks students to engage in reading not graphic novel panels but advertisements. This is because we have found ads an effective way to engage students while demonstrating how a well-designed image can relay and often manipulate a specific message for a targeted audience.

LESSON: VISUAL LITERACY ASSESSMENT

Mastery Objective. Evaluating students' understanding of visual literacy and their visual literacy skills.

Materials Needed

▣ Visual Literacy Assessment Rubric (shown later in this lesson).

Note: you can find the Visual Literacy Assesment Rubric in a reproducible format on our websites (www.wiley.com/go/worthathousandwords; meryljaffe.com; and taliahurwich.com)

▣ *Optional*: white paper and coloring utensils.

Introducing the Lesson

▣ **Individual Work.** For homework or as an in-class assignment, have students draw or create an advertisement for a new toy, for some community service, for their favorite vacation spot, or for anything they want.

   They can create the ad by drawing it, by using online tools, or by making a collage from magazine images.

▣ **Individual Presentations.** Once the ads are completed, have each student present his or her ad.

Note that after each presentation, you may want to ask guided questions, to get a more complete picture of each student's visual literacy skills. To adequately evaluate their visual literacy skills for this activity, you need to assess the following:

   ▣ What students thought the ad should say and do.

   ▣ How they designed the ad to do and say what they wanted it to.

   ▣ How effective the design elements were.

   ▣ How their message resonated with their audience, both culturally and emotionally.

   For example, you may want to push them to say why they used certain colors, why they selected the slogan they did, and why they used the images they did, and the like.

▣ **Assessment.** As they present their ads, you may want to use the following visual literacy assessment rubric we've created to evaluate their visual literacy skills.

Visual Literacy Assessment Rubric

Student Name_____

Component	Basic skills: Student notices compositional components	Proficient: Student recognizes the effect of the artist's choices	Advanced: Student generates alternative options or choices

Shapes
 	
Student
 	
    recognizes the use of different shapes to hold our attention;
 	
    compares how the shapes are used in the image to how they're frequently seen in everyday life; and
 	
    connects a shape to a commonly associated emotion.
 	
(For example, circles tend to feel "inclusive"; multifaceted shapes with jagged edges may feel "dangerous," and the like)			

Icons Student recognizes/discusses the use of icons and symbols within the image. (For example, if someone is inside a bubble, that bubble may represent a barrier; bright flowers flowing everywhere may represent spring or happiness or joviality, and the like)			

Fonts
 	
Student recognizes/discusses fonts in terms of
 	
    shapes;
 	
    sizes; and/or
 	
    changes in font reflecting emotions or actions.			

Facial features Student recognizes how the eyes, mouth, forehead, and/or facial expressions of the characters reflect their feelings/emotions/ reactions.			

(continued)

29

Component	Basic skills: Student notices compositional components	Proficient: Student recognizes the effect of the artist's choices	Advanced: Student generates alternative options or choices
Color Student recognizes the (different) uses of colors in the image content and design to hold our attention; compares how the colors are used in the image to how they're frequently seen in everyday life; and connects a specific color to a commonly associated emotion. (For example, red might signify danger; green may reflect nature; blue may be calm like the sky, and so forth)			
Shading Student recognizes the (different) uses of shading in the image to hold our attention and to relay action; and connects the use of shading to a commonly associated emotion. (For example, dashes and shading behind a character's foot may indicate walking or running; a lot of hashes may reflect tension or anger, and the like)			
Perspective Student recognizes the angle of the "shot" of the image and its action. (For example, whether the viewer is embedded within or invited into the scene, or is separated and uninvited; whether it's a close-up or a wide-angle view; whether it's an aerial or high-angle view making the characters look smaller or a low-angle view making them look larger and empowered, and so forth)			
Layout/design Student recognizes where or upon what her or his eye initially focuses; where the main action is (usually foreground); and important but secondary details (usually midground/background).			

Assessment Rubric Directions. Use this rubric to evaluate students' visual literacy pre-lesson, as suggested earlier or for any other assessment that relies on interpreting images. Note that this form can be used to evaluate students' written work or a class discussion.

Keep in mind that regardless of their age or skill, when discussing visual literacy for the first time, your students may need prompting. They may understand, for example, how color influences our emotions but may not think to mention it in a discussion. Hence some prompting may be necessary (at least initially).

When evaluating students' written critiques of visual images and for older students, you may want to create a sheet for each student and record comments they've made in appropriate boxes and/or simply check off what they observe, understand, and/or have mastered.

When evaluating visual literacy assessment discussions and for younger students (not yet capable of critically responding in a written format), you may want to use one sheet, recording student names in the boxes reflecting who was able to observe, understand, and or master each of the rubric elements.

This Assessment: Understanding What to Expect Developmentally

This assessment activity and the assessment rubric were designed for students of all ages. Student competency skills will depend on developmental as well as cognitive and language skills.

What to Expect from Students of All Ages

All students should be able to do the following:

- Recognize what in the image is relaying action; what is relaying reaction or emotion. For example:
  - lines or dashes behind someone's feet (often seen in comics) indicates the person is walking or running; and
  - different facial and body features relay emotions (such as "happy," "angry," "scared," or "embarrassed").
- Recognize that compositional elements are intentionally chosen to influence us. For example:
  - the images authors choose (for example, why they use a talking bear, or a famous entertainer, or a bubbling brook, and the like);
  - the color and shading choices;
  - the perspective and angles from which we view an image; and
  - the text choices and the text font and size choices.

- Recognize that while images tell stories and relay information, they *also* play upon and relay emotions.
- Look at an image and use visual evidence to justify how a character has been made to look happy, friendly, scared, angry, aggressive, and so on.
- Discuss the use of color and how it makes the reader feel.
- Recognize how the angle or perspective influences the "shot" – whether the viewer is
  - eye level, as if to be included and invited into the scene;
  - looking down from above, and not necessarily included but possibly more empowered;
  - looking from below, and less empowered;
  - viewing from close up, and more invited; or
  - viewing from a wide-angle shot, as an observer rather than a participant.

What to Expect from Older Students

Older students (grades 3 or 4+) should be able to do the following:

- Recognize the cultural influence color choice plays. For example:
  - red often relays danger;
  - yellow suggests caution;
  - blue is calming;
  - purple often reflects royalty or opulence;
  - black may relay exclusivity or destruction; and
  - green often reflects nature or being natural.
- Recognize the artist's use of symbols and icons. For example:
  - the way characters are drawn (i.e. stick figures, cartoon figures, real-life figures, anthropomorphic animals or plants, and so on);
  - religious symbols;
  - cultural references and icons;
  - environmental markers (i.e. universal road signs such as "Stop," "Yield," and "Caution").
- Recognize how shading, lines, texture, and color relay actions, concepts, and emotions.
- Recognize how foreground, midground, and background are manipulated by an artist to highlight certain actions, events, and/or emotions and to obscure others.
- Justify why they liked specific choices the artist made, and why they did not like others.
- Justify why the specific items that appeal to them may not appeal to others.

Teaching Visual Literacy Skills to Your Students

Once the assessments are graded or reviewed, you'll have a good idea of how visually aware and literate your students are. Now you'll be able to more effectively use and tweak the visual literacy lesson presented in this section, which involves critically reading an iconic (community service) advertisement.

In this lesson we provide a Smokey the Bear ad (the original ad) for you to discuss and reflect upon with your students. We've chosen this ad because it can be used for all ages, and because it has been an incredibly successful ad, as Smokey Bear has been teaching the public about wildfire prevention since 1944.

Background Information About the Smokey the Bear Ad

Following this ad's initial success, songwriters Steve Nelson and Jack Rollins wrote the successful song "Smokey the Bear" (1952), and Ideal Toys vended a Smokey Bear doll. In the 1955 Little Golden Book *Smokey the Bear*, Smokey told his story; and in the 1969–1970 television season, Rankin/Bass produced *The Smokey the Bear Show*, a weekly Saturday morning series, for ABC. Even today, Smokey Bear has his own Facebook page (smokeybear.com) with games, lessons, and resources for school and home fun.

Modeling a Critical Discussion Around the Ad

When modeling how to critically read and discuss the Smokey Bear advertisement you may want to make sure you include the following points:

- In the original ad, we see a picture of Smokey dressed in jeans and a Ranger's hat bending over a campfire and putting it out using a bucket of water. Around Smokey (in the foreground), we see drying brush or grass in what appears to be a camping field. There's a mature forest surrounding the field in the background.

- We notice Smokey painstakingly bent over dousing the fire (with plumes of smoke rising upward, as flames still dance around the water). This act reflects the concern and care he takes. Interestingly, however, while he is bent down his one visible eye is not really looking at the fire, it's looking at us. We recognize that he's talking to us, hoping to engage us while asking us to help by caring.

- Smokey Bear's clothing (Ranger's hat and working clothes) relays his authority to spearhead the campaign. He doesn't just talk and teach about wildfire prevention, he actually works to save his forest(s).

- Finally, regarding the use of colors, the image of Smokey and his forest is in natural earth colors (browns – both bold and muted, blues, and greens) and it is surrounded by a black frame containing orange-colored text. On the one hand, the browns and blues are colors that are soothing and natural. On the other hand, Smokey's message, framed and separated from the image, is in black with large, bold, orange color text. As a result it stands out and is somewhat jarring. The image of the forest is relaxing, reflecting nature at its best. Smokey's message is neither natural nor soothing. The text color and size, the exclamation point, and the underlined word demand our attention.

VISUAL LITERACY LESSON DETAILS: CRITICALLY READING IMAGES (ALL AGES)

Mastery Objective. Students will discover how to critically read and discuss an image by analyzing its content, its use of color, how it's framed, the perspective chosen by the artist, and the moments in time depicted.

Materials Needed

The Smokey the Bear debut advertisement in Figure 3.2, or any other advertisement that you feel may resonate more with your students from a magazine, newspaper, or online resource.

Note: this Smokey the Bear advertisement can be found in a reproducible format on our websites (www.wiley.com/go/worthathousandwords, meryljaffe.com, and talia-hurwich.com)

Materials you would like your students to use when creating their own advertisements.

Optional "Who's My Author" worksheet.

FIGURE 3.2   Smokey the Bear advertisement
Source: South Dakota Department of Agriculture, *History of Smokey Bear*, http://sdda. sd.gov/legacydocs/forestry/ educational-information/pdf/ history-of-smokeybear.pdf.

Note that if you're interested in building a unit around this advertisement, or simply introducing the ad, the Smokey Bear website at smokeybear.com/en/smokeys-history/

story-of-smokey discusses the campaign's history as well as the story of Smokey Bear (a bear cub rescued from a devastating forest fire), the history of the Smokey Bear campaign, and how the campaign has changed over time. This link also has teaching resources for elementary and middle school classrooms as well as suggested forest and conservation links. Finally, this ad is a public service announcement, and you might want to follow up your discussion of this ad by creating your own class public service announcement.

Introducing the Lesson

- Discuss what students like about the advertisement and what they don't like.

- *Optional*. You may want to give a brief history of the Smokey Bear campaign.

- Introduce the concept that *everything* in this advertisement was chosen on purpose, and intended to influence the people who see the ad.

Guided Practice (a whole class activity)

Have a mini-scavenger hunt, asking students these questions as you create a four-column list on the board detailing their responses:

- What's in the image? or, What do we see?

- What isn't in the image? or, What don't we see?

- What's surprising?

- What's communicated in the image and text?

Make sure you discuss these issues:

- Why Smokey is in the foreground;

- Why Smokey is doing what he's doing;

- Why Smokey is wearing a Ranger's hat and blue jeans;

- Why Smokey and his forest are drawn in blues, greens, and browns, while the text on the bottom (outside the picture of the forest) is in a bold black frame with bold orange lettering; also, why the text is punctuated the way it is;

- How this particular ad is used to influence the viewer; and

- How effective the ad and its overt and implied messages are.

For homework or in class, have students select two advertisements. One they like and think is convincing, and one they don't like. (They will need them for Phase 1 of their independent practice.)

Independent Practice

Materials Needed. Use the advertisements students found.

(continued)

Student Instructions for Phase 1 (in pairs or small groups)

- Discuss what you like about the "successful" ads you chose.

- Analyze the artistic choices and details included that make the ad successful.

- Discuss what you don't like about the "unsuccessful" ads you chose.

- Analyze what it is you don't like and why the choices don't seem to work.

Student Instructions for Phase 2 (individually)

- Create your own advertisement.

Optional Unit Assessment and Debrief

Using the visual literacy assessment rubric, evaluate students' advertisements and how successful they were with the choices they made. Compare pre-lesson to post-lesson performances. When handing back graded work, discuss students' performance, highlighting essential points and reviewing any elements they appeared to have difficulty with (see the issues to discuss in the guided practice section for details you may want to review).

Alternate or Final Visual Literacy Assessment Exercise

Have students find, choose, or create an image that they feel best represents who they are. Have them explain, discuss, or write how and why their image's specific content and design best relays their message.

Once students' images are completed, hang these visual messages up (making sure there are no names on the images). Have the class "promenade," looking at and evaluating each image. Have them try to guess who created each image, noting why they made those choices. Following the promenade, discuss their work and why their best guesses were correct or incorrect. You may want to give each student a copy of the Who's My Author student assessment worksheet to record his or her reactions.

Note: this assessment can be found in a reproducible format on our websites (www.wiley. com/go/worthathousandwords, meryljaffe.com, and taliahurwich.com)

Who's My Author: Visual Literacy Assessment Exercise – Assessment of Student Worksheet

Student Name _____

Poster description	Author: Best guess	Rationale for your guess

For a shorter lesson, have each student present her or his image, and have the others constructively critique how effectively the image actually relays its intended message.

Moving On

At this point, you and your students should be ready to move on to learning how to critically read
graphic novels. In the next chapter, we take you and your students from smaller to larger presentations. We begin by exploring a graphic novel's "anatomy," reflecting upon and integrating the
parts played by its panels, text, frames, and page design. We then provide a lesson for you to use
with your students as you monitor their understanding of a graphic novel's basic elements.

FOUNDATIONAL SKILLS IN GRAPHIC NOVELS, PART 2
HOW TO TEACH GRAPHIC NOVELS

Once you've established and assessed your students' skills in reading images, you're ready to move on to teaching them how to critically read graphic novels. In this chapter, we relate graphic novels' essential elements along with strategies and insights to best build your students' comprehension and graphic novel toolbox. Finally, we provide lesson suggestions and additional resources to make your classroom graphic novel units as meaningful and effective as possible.

As we hope we've impressed upon you, the most important element to keep in mind when reading graphic novels is that everything on the page is intentional. The images, text, panel and page design, what's included and what's not included, are all chosen to relay content. Comprehension involves incorporating both verbal and visual literacies. So once you've established your students' visual literacy, you are ready to use, incorporate, and enjoy graphic novels.

Before proceeding however, we want to convey that we've had many years of practice in reading and integrating graphic novels into our classrooms, and accordingly, we provide and model a good amount of depth for you to assimilate and use – without, we hope, over-whelming the beginners among our readers. We therefore encourage you to explore your own comfort level as you go through this chapter while considering the needs and skills of your students. You know your students' skills better than anyone and are best equipped to deter-mine where to start and what level of depth and details to effectively engage. It is our goal to provide you with insights and resources to best empower you for making the necessary adjustments as you meet your students' diverse learning styles and needs. So with all this in mind – *let's begin!*

We first identify key graphic novel terms and elements. In order to effectively teach with this format, you and your students will need a common vocabulary with which to discuss and communicate critical details. While older students may be familiar with most if not all of these terms, younger students may not. We suggest using Figure 4.1, which shows the anatomy of a graphic novel, as a reference for your students or as an introduction to the suggested lessons in this chapter. Then we relate how authors use each of these essential elements to relay their stories. We complete this chapter with sample lessons.

So to begin, let's discuss key graphic novel components. These include panels, panel frames, various types of text balloons, and gutters, as illustrated in Figure 4.1, using a page from Raina Telgemeier's *Smile* to help us.

Note: Figure 4.1 can be found in a reproducible format on our websites (www.wiley.com/go/worthathousandwords, meryljaffe.com, and taliahurwich.com)

FIGURE 4.1 Anatomy of a graphic novel
Source: Raina Telgemeier, *Smile* (New York: Scholastic, 2010), p. 16.

The Anatomy of a Graphic Novel: Panels

Panels are graphic novels' building blocks. Their shape, content, viewing angle, frames, text, and various text balloons relay story elements.

Panel Shapes

Panel shapes often vary from page to page and from graphic novel to graphic novel, although typically they are rectangular. Panel shapes differ in an effort to set a pace and rhythm for the story, to maintain reader interest, and to relay subtle information.

- Squares and rectangles may signify symmetry, straightness, and/or stability.

- Triangular shapes may signify escalating violence, energy, or activity or deescalating violence, energy, or activity, depending on where the apex is.

- Circular shapes may signify endlessness, protection, and/or inclusiveness.

- Diamond shapes may be used to grab our attention and/or illustrate the centrality of the contents inside.

Panel Sizes

Panel sizes also vary from page to page. A panel's size can relate to whether the panel provides overviews or details (much like a wide-angle perspective versus a close-up). Different sizes may be used to emphasize or highlight key events, details and/or emotions, which in turn influences the pace and rhythm of the storytelling. For example:

- A small panel may be used to relate background information, or to emphasize or direct us to focus on an intimate or pivotal moment or an essential element. Small panels may be imbedded in larger ones, or they may stand alone, drawing our attention to an important detail.

- A large panel typically provides a wider angle, offering us an overview of a particular location or event, establishing the shot, escalating an action, or setting the tone.

Figure 4.2 illustrates how panel shapes and sizes help to tell a story. It's taken from *Saints* – part of the two-book set *Boxers and Saints* by Gene Luen Yang. *Boxers* recounts the Chinese Boxer Rebellion from the Chinese peasants' perspective, while *Saints* recounts the Christians' perspective.

The opening panel of Figure 4.2 is what is frequently called "the establishing shot." It is a bit larger than most of the other panels to give us time to reflect upon this new scene. The second panel, focusing on the character's face, is smaller and more intimate. This gives the reader a chance to more closely infer what's going on in her head. The third panel is large occupying one third of the page. It spans the page's width and demands our attention as we quickly recognize that it's a dramatic moment (from both the exclamation mark in the text balloon and the introduction of the two golden figures). Finally, the bottom third of the page contains even smaller rectangular

FIGURE 4.2 Panel shapes and sizes in *Boxers and Saints*
Source: Gene Luen Yang, *Saints* (New York: First Second, 2013), p. 55.

panels. These panels slow us down to emphasize the importance of the moment, focusing individually on each character's reaction, making sure that we understand the depth of what's going on. These reflections about panel size are then confirmed and strengthened by reading the content found within the panels' frames.

Panel Frames

Panel frames are optional lines that surround the panels. Typically panels have some type of frame. When panels are framed, the frame typically consists of some sort of line around the panel.

FIGURE 4.3 Bleed across panel frame in *Space Dumplins*
Source: Craig Thompson, *Space Dumplins* (New York: Scholastic Graphix, 2015), p. 83.

Sometimes, however, scalloped lines are used to depict a flashback, a dream, and/or a thought. In some instances however a panel may have no frame. This is often done to draw our attention to a pivotal action, emotion, or moment.

Finally, there are instances when some object in the panel protrudes or "bleeds" through the frame. This is usually done to show that some violent or extreme action or emotion is so strong it can't be contained. Consider, for example, the page from *Space Dumplins*, by Craig Thompson, in Figure 4.3. Notice how, in the top right panel, the robot babysitter's arm extends out of the frame to tape Violet's foul mouth. Later, in the final panel, the robot babysitter gets so angry, her blinding lights bleed through the panel's frame as she shuts up Zacchareus (Zee for short), who with the robot babysitter's action is lifted out of her carriage and also extends through the frame. From the content, what comes across is a humorous moment. However, by bleeding through the frames, the size and sheer presence of the babysitter is emphasized – she literally cannot fit into the scene. Furthermore, the asymmetry of her breaking the frame at the bottom is uncomfortable. This isn't supposed to make us feel like the drama has ended. Instead, it pulls our eyes to the literal edge of the paper and begs us to flip the page.

To review or assess your students' understanding of panels and panel frames, you may want to use the following lesson.

LESSON: PANEL AND PANEL FRAMES

Mastery Objective. Students will explore various panel and panel frame format options in an effort to better understand them.

Materials Needed

Graphic novel panels that are *not framed*. Make sure you have a varied selection of panels showing action, daydreaming, thoughts, close-ups, intense actions and reactions, flashbacks, and the like.

Introducing the Lesson

- Show students a selection of graphic novel pages (including but not limited to ones like Figure 4.3).
- Discuss how panel frames may differ and why (to keep images interesting; to differentiate present moments from flashbacks or dreams; to show intense action or emotion; etc.). Critique and evaluate favorite and least favorite panels, and discuss how panel frame shapes help the storytelling and the reading experience.
- Explain to students that for this lesson they will be creating, experimenting with, and evaluating different types of panel frames.

Independent or Group Practice

Pass out an unframed panel or image to each student or student group, with the following instructions.

Student Instructions

With your panel, you are going to do the following:

- On a sheet of paper, write down all the possible story lines you think the panel or image is telling.
- Choose the story line you like best, and frame the panel or image in a way that best highlights that story line.
- Once everyone's finished, you'll all present your framed panel or image, explaining
  - the story line you're following;
  - the framing options you thought about; and
  - why you chose the framing option that you did.

Lesson Simplification for Younger Students

Hand out a panel to a group of students along with different types of frames you've created (e.g., straight line frame, scalloped line frame, circular frame, etc.). Have them select the frame that best fits the panel. Then, when they're sharing their frame choices, make sure they explain

- what is going on in the panel; and

- why they chose the frame that they chose.

Lesson Debrief and Assessment (for all grades)

Once each student or group has presented and discussed their panel and frame choice, discuss with them how the different framing options influence the meaning and/or the experience of reading the image. Base assessments on the content of their group work and their comments or discussions.

The Anatomy of a Graphic Novel: Narrative, Text, and Thought Balloons

Balloons (also referred to as bubbles) are typically found inside panels and contain the story's text. Balloons may be of various types:

- **Narrative or staging balloons** inform readers and set the stage for changes in the plot, character perspectives, conflict, and/or setting. They're often set in rectangular boxes at the top of the panel, may be a different color from the text balloons, and may use a font different from that used for dialogue.

- **Text or dialogue balloons** relay what a character says aloud.

- **Thought balloons** relate a character's thoughts, emotions, and motives. They're typically drawn with wavy or scalloped lines, or they may have small balloons connecting the character to the thought.

- **Sound-effect balloons** relate sound, usually via large and interesting fonts and/or colors.

Figure 4.4 is a sample page of various balloon shapes and functions taken from *Squish: Super Amoeba* by Jennifer Holm and Matthew Holm. What's so interesting in *Squish* (and *Babymouse*, another series by Jennifer and Matthew Holm) is that the narrator (with a wonderfully snarky personality) has an active role interacting with the characters as well as the reader. To help the readers distinguish the character dialogue, the narrator dialogue, the narrative, and sound effects from one another, the Holms use varied balloon styles and/or colors.

To review or assess your students' understanding of various text balloons, you may want to use the following lesson, "Text Balloons."

FIGURE 4.4 Use of text balloons of varying styles in *Squish: Super Amoeba*
Source: Matthew Holm and Jennifer Holm, *Squish: Super Amoeba* (New York: Random House, 2011), p. 33.

LESSON: TEXT BALLOONS (ALL GRADES)

Mastery Objective. Students will explore the different ways text is presented in a given scene's text balloons in an effort to better understand these devices.

Materials Needed

- Figure 4.1 ("Anatomy of a Graphic Novel") and/or Figure 4.4 ("Use of Text Balloons of Varying Styles in *Squish: Super Amoeba*"), or an appropriate page from any other graphic novel of your choice, to display or to give to students as a handout. In this lesson we describe how you might use Figure 4.1.

- Various scenes from moments in time (history, fairy tales, familiar stories, or the like); each scene listed on an individual index card. (You will use one card for the guided practice and the others will be selected or given to each group during the independent practice.) Scenes may include

- the Three Little Pigs facing the Wolf's final assault in the last pig's brick house;

- a kid catching the Tooth Fairy in action;

- two birds and a cockroach resting in the Liberty Bell Tower as the bell is rung in 1776;

- soldiers crossing the Delaware with General George Washington in the dead of winter as they run from the Red Coats;

- a family riding in a wagon train heading West . . . it's been four months . . .;

- Jack climbing down the beanstalk with the singing harp in hand and the Giant close behind;

- a family traveling in the first nonmilitary shuttle to Mars, for a vacation; and/or

- blank cards for students to create their own scenes.

- *For younger students* have a collection of empty text balloons of various shapes and frames for them to use when recreating the scene(s) they're given.

- *For older students* have blank paper, colored pens, and scissors for them to use to design the various text balloons for their scene(s).

Introducing the Lesson

- Using Figure 4.1 ("Anatomy of a Graphic Novel") ask students to comment on how Ms. Telgemeier relays dialogue, narrative, and characters' thoughts.

- Discuss how authors may design and use various text balloons and how the shapes differ to help readers recognize and distinguish narrative, dialogue, and thought.

- Once students have a clear idea on how to use text balloons, tell them that they will now have an opportunity to create their own text balloons for a selected scene.

Guided Practice (a whole class activity)

Take one of the index cards you've prepared and read aloud the scene you've selected. Pause for a few moments, asking students to quietly think about it. More specifically, have them think about what the characters might say, what they might think, and what sounds they might hear.

After the students have had a few moments to think, first ask them what the characters might say. Write their suggestions in a dialogue balloon on the board.

Then ask what sound effect the characters might be thinking. Write that on the board. Ask how an artist might frame that in a thought balloon.

(continued)

47

Next, ask students what the characters might hear, and how an artist might frame the balloon so others would know this is a sound effect.

Select the dialogue and sound effect balloons you think work best for the scene. Have students volunteer to read or act out the text balloons selected. Ask if readers would immediately know what was going on, or if they might need some direction from a narrator to help figure out what was going on. Discuss how that text balloon might look.

Optional. Select students to come up and reenact the scene again – one student for each character, one student for the narrator, and one student for each sound effect.

Debrief. Ask students how effective their text selections and text balloon choices were. What worked? What didn't work?

Independent or Group Practice

Explain that you will now break the class into groups. Each group will select an index card with a scene they must create text balloons for. Just like the process you've just done together.

It will be the students' job to take that moment in time and recreate the dialogue, sound effects, narrative, and/or characters' thoughts for that moment. For younger students, we recommend you provide pre-made, empty dialogue, narrative, and sound effect balloons. For older students, you may want them to create their own various text balloons.

Once the groups are finished, each group will then be assigned the text balloons from a different group. Each group will enact the scene and try to guess what it is. That way everyone will be able to see how effective the text balloons were.

Note that while having pre-created scenes for younger students is highly recommended, you may want to offer older students an opportunity to create their own scenes.

Alternate Independent or Group Practice

Pass out the scene cards.

Have students create text balloons to best reenact the scene(s).

Once students are finished creating their text balloons have them number each balloon to represent the order in which they should be read.

Once the balloons are ordered and numbered, have each group reenact their scene by reading or acting out their text balloons. After each presentation ask the audience what that scene was.

You may want to ask the group presenting the scene how challenging it was to create, select, and order their text balloons.

Lesson Debrief and Assessment

Once each student or group has presented and discussed their text balloon choice(s), discuss and critique. Assess how effective each group's text balloon choices were in relaying the designated scene.

Gutters

Gutters are the spaces between panels. They serve two purposes: they signify points of transition (from one sequential piece of the story to another), and as such points, they provide opportunities for reflection. Authors cannot possibly supply every second or thought or event that takes place during a story. As a result, readers must fill in the missing gaps. That's done in the gutters, and while it doesn't necessarily merit a teaching moment, much as with the space between paragraphs, this is where you monitor comprehension. One more thing to note about gutters is that they may change in the course of the storytelling. When this occurs, it too may merit discussion.

Figure 4.5, a page from *March: Book One*, is just one example of how gutters can vary. As you can see, the fourth panel is an unframed panel. As a result, you can't distinguish where the

FIGURE 4.5 Use of varied gutters in *March: Book One*
Source: John Lewis, Andrew Ayden, and Nate Powell, *March: Book One*
(Marietta, GA: Top Shelf Productions, 2013), p. 41.

gutters begin and end and where the frameless panel begins and ends. These changes grab readers' attention and merit reflection:

- *Why* is this happening here – as they're entering Ohio?

- *Why* are there no distinguishing frames or borders – what are the authors telling us, and what are they asking us to consider?

Note that whenever discussing changes one notices in a particular panel, frame, gutter, or page format, the question really is "what does this change mean to me?" As points of reflection, they are open to individuals' interpretations and, as such, they often make for interesting and insightful discussions.

For those interested, in learning more about gutters, Scott McCloud's *Understanding Comics: The Invisible Art* (Harper, 1993, pp. 60–93) provides a detailed discussion of different types of panel transitions. It's well worth a read.

LESSON: ASSESSING STUDENTS' UNDER-STANDING OF GRAPHIC NOVEL ANATOMY

Mastery Objective. Assess students' understanding of graphic novel anatomy.

Materials Needed

- Figure 4.1: "Anatomy of a Graphic Novel."

- Figure 4.5: Page 41 from *March: Book One* by John Lewis, Andrew Ayden, and Nate Powell, 2013.

- Poster boards.

- A collection of graphic novels to examine (in your class, school, or local library).

Introducing the Lesson

- Review your discussions about panels and text balloons.

- Discuss one final aspect of graphic novels – their gutters.

- You may want to use Figure 4.1 "Anatomy of a Graphic Novel," when discussing how Ms. Telgemeier uses her panels. Then show the students Figure 4.5 and discuss the use of gutters there. Discuss how the different uses of gutters affect or influence the storytelling.

- Tell students that they will now be putting all the graphic novel pieces together. They'll be creating their own one-page graphic novel stories, where they'll have to create and decide upon panel shapes, panel frames, text balloons, and gutters.

Group Practice

Assign six groups of students.

Give each student group a poster board and an assigned graphic novel component: panel, panel frame, narrative balloon, dialogue balloon, thought balloon, or gutter.

Student Instructions

On your poster board, I want you to demonstrate what your assigned component is. Illustrate where you would find it on a graphic novel page, and provide examples of at least two different forms it might take in any given instance. For example, if you are doing frames, draw different types of frames. If you're doing panels, discuss the panel elements and how they might differ from panel to panel. If you're doing gutters or balloons, show how they may vary and use the specific terminology (i.e. a "narrative balloon" or "dialogue balloon") for the designated balloon.

Once the Poster Boards Are Finished

Have students use the classroom, school, or local library to select their favorite example of their assigned component.

Then, when all students are meeting together as a class, have each group explain the dynamics of their component as illustrated on their poster board, and explain why they selected their favorite example.

Lesson Debrief (for all grades)

Once each student or group has presented and discussed favorite graphic novel examples, discuss these choices. Does everyone have the same taste? Why or why not?

Putting This All Together and Taking a Page for a Spin

At this point you and your students should be ready to critically read graphic novels. In this section we do three things, while going from smaller to larger presentations. First, in Figure 4.6, we will take a panel for a spin, referring back to our discussion of *March: Book One* in Chapter 3 and answering the questions posed there and provided again in the next section of this chapter. Once you've reviewed your notes and our comments for Figure 4.6, the next step is to take the page for a spin, reflecting on and integrating the parts played by its panels, text, frames, and page design. Please refer back to Figure 4.5 as well for this discussion. To close this section, we provide a lesson for you to use with your students as you monitor their understanding of a graphic novel's basic elements.

Critically Reading a Panel

Looking again at the top panel from page 27 of *March: Book One* in Figure 4.6, consider once more the questions posed earlier:

- What jumps out at you?
- What surprises you in terms of what is or is not in the image?
- Why is text relayed in different fonts and font sizes?
- What is being communicated in the images and text? What are we expected to infer from the images and text?

The first thing we notice in Figure 4.6 is a black silhouetted figure, filled with a passage etched in white text, sitting on a very simple porch, and hunched over a book. We are surprised by this dramatic text-filled figure. Next, we're struck by the panel's overall composition, perspective, lack of a frame, and the much smaller inserted panels of the chicken coop. With this open (borderless) image we feel as if we're invited there as Lewis ponders a particularly

FIGURE 4.6 Panel from *March: Book One*
Source: John Lewis, Andrew Ayden, and Nate Powell, *March: Book One* (Marietta, GA: Top Shelf Productions, 2013), p. 27.

troubling Bible passage and preaches to his flock. While we're drawn first to the larger frameless panel, it's the smaller panels that are used to give us more background and that set up the scene to follow.

After Lewis's dark black figure and the porch he's sitting on draw us in, we notice the remaining images are etched in light gray strokes. The bottom part of a post next to Lewis (with jagged edges on top) infers that there's an overhang or roof protecting him from Alabama's harsh summer sun. Furthermore, the lighter strokes of blacks and greys at the edge of the porch are used to show us the simplicity of the Lewis's front porch and background.

Then we realize details that are missing. We notice that the porch has no railing implying that it's nothing fancy. Furthermore there are no details, no grass, no crops, no nothing around Lewis or the porch, inferring that the field and grounds around the house were not as important to Lewis or that the land was barren. What we see are the chickens below – Lewis's flock, to which he preached the Bible's lessons. What we infer from this is that the Bible is what grabs Lewis's attention (and ours), particularly the one phrase that "struck him strongly." It's literally etched in his very being. We also notice that Lewis's head, book, and leg protrude from their confined space, implying that the passage on his back is boundless, powerful, and as much a part of his being as his body and clothes are.

Taking a Page for a Spin: Critically Reading a Whole Page (from its panels to its page design)

Keeping the previous section in mind, let's expand our critical reading to the full page from *March: Book One* displayed in Figure 4.5. On this page, we see young John Lewis traveling north with his Uncle Otis from Lewis's home in Alabama. Uncle Otis is taking Lewis to spend the summer in the cooler and somewhat safer city of Chicago. We know from the preceding pages that driving was often quite dangerous. Blacks were not allowed to stop at white stores or allowed to use white facilities. We also know there have been incidents that Uncle Otis and Lewis hope to avoid.

The first thing you may notice is that the five panels on this page are similarly shaped. Each panel is rectangular and splashed horizontally across the page. However, there are some very noticeable differences as well. Some of the panels have complete borders, some have partial borders, and one has no border. Some panels are smaller – almost the size of a rear-view mirror – and others are larger and open, as if inviting us into the car with Lewis and Uncle Otis. Each panel also has a very different perspective as it moves the story along. Also, notice the impact of the gutters on this page. As the panels are clear, distinct snapshots of moments in the car, the gutters are essential. We need them to separate the these snapshots that reflect the different moments in time and locations along the characters' drive, while allowing us to fill in what's missing. Let's take a closer look.

Panel 1

Panel 1 is a bird's-eye view of a bridge. There's a rectangular narrative text balloon above the bridge, which spans the panel. We see a car, we presume it's their car, in the bottom left corner of the panel. It's trailing dust behind. We're told, "It wasn't until we got into Ohio" – we're left hanging, wondering what it is that happened in Ohio. But we don't have to wait long. Note that the bridge also serves as a metaphor, "bridging" the difference between the hostile South and the more tolerant North.

Panel 2

Panel 2 is a close-up of Uncle Otis's chest. It's a fascinating choice of image and one not to be taken for granted. This close-up shows us the palpable tension felt in the car. What's wonderfully intriguing in this panel is the dissonance between the wording and the image. While we're told, "that I could feel Uncle Otis relax," we clearly see that's not happening . . . yet. We're inside the car with Lewis and Uncle Otis and (intentionally) a bit too close for comfort. All we see is that Uncle Otis's shirt is buttoned and his tie is tied as he sits driving with both hands on the steering wheel (they're both raised a bit although all we see is his left-hand thumb on the top part of the wheel). This panel's dissonance adds a tension that propels the conflict and the story forward.

Panel 3

Panel 3 is another close up. Otis and Lewis are still inside the car, and now we're incredibly close up and very uncomfortable. All we see are Uncle Otis's eyes and brow. He's looking intently to the left. His eyes are narrowed, focused. Sweat is dripping from his brow. We can feel his fear and trepidation as he's driving – still in the South – and still afraid of trouble.

Panel 4

Panel 4 is a frameless image of a car (Otis's car) zipping past the sign "You are now entering OHIO The Buckeye State Welcomes All." This is the only frameless image on the page, which demands our attention and begs the question: Why is *this* panel borderless? In our opinion, it's frameless because this is a pivotal moment. It marks the transition from danger to safety. It marks the point where Lewis and Uncle Otis can relax and breathe easier.

Panel 5

Panel 5 is a close-up – although not as close as the other two. We are face to face with young John and Uncle Otis. We are inside the car with them, but at a more comfortable distance. John tells us he finally relaxed too, and we see the two men in the front seat, stuff piled behind them. The bridge we saw at the top of the page is far in the distant hills. Uncle Otis's eyes are larger, rounder. He has unbuttoned the top button of his shirt and is loosening his tie with his left hand while driving with his right. (We now have one clear reason why we saw the close-up of Uncle Otis's chest and shirt earlier.) John is gazing out the window. We're not sure what he's thinking about but it doesn't really matter. The danger is gone. Not only are we told they relaxed, we can see it. We can feel it.

LESSON: GETTING COMFORTABLE WITH PANEL AND PAGE COMPONENTS (ALL AGES).

In this lesson, we recommend you select or have your students create a "class" story. It should be a simple story that you'll write in prose and then have your students create a comic/graphic novel rendition of it. This lesson is all about integrating and better understanding the types of choices the students need to consider when creating their own graphic novels or comics or when critically reading them.

Mastery Objective. Students will gain deeper understanding of a graphic novel's basic components by integrating, designing, and creating their own components from (very) short stories.

Materials Needed

- A short and simple, predetermined (prose) story (or poem).

- Unlined paper, a ruler, pencils – regular pencils and/or colored pencils (crayons optional).

Introducing the Lesson

- Review how graphic novels work. You may want to look back at the "Anatomy of a Graphic Novel" lesson earlier in this chapter.

- Tell your students that now, having mastered the different parts of a graphic novel, they will tell their own stories in graphic novel format.

Guided Practice

Inform students that they'll be taking a very short text, poem, or story and transforming it into a mini–graphic novel.

Present (or create) the prose text, making sure it is short and fairly simple. You may want to construct a very short story together with the students, or to save time, you may want to simply select one for your students to transform.

Note that the story, poem, or text must be simple so students will have an easier time balancing text and image in their graphic novels. Their decision on how much text to include will depend on the story or poem selected.

Introduce the independent practice element of the lesson, where the students will be creating their own rendition of the prose text you just created or introduced. You may want to show an example of transforming text to image, either by taking an action sentence

(continued)

and transforming it into a panel or by showing text from a prose story (such as *Ember City*, *The Golden Compass*, *Nursery Rhymes*, or *Trickster Tales*) with the corresponding pages from a graphic novel rendition of that story. Discuss the use of text and how to select what (and how much) text to use and why.

Independent Practice

Have students create their own mini-graphic novel of the very short story or poem you've selected or created.

Discuss how they might balance image in relation to text. Discuss decisions on using color versus black and white, and any other choices you may wish to help them with.

Once students are finished with their creations, post their work for all to see.

Once the works have been viewed, discuss and critique how they are similar or different and why. Discuss what seems to work best and why. Discuss what doesn't seem to work and why.

Assessment

Evaluate students' mini-graphic novels in terms of how successful they were with the choices made for panel design, for break down and use of text, and for the rhythm and flow of the panels (page design).

Alternate Lesson (all ages)

Select a page from any graphic novel appropriate for your students' ages and reading level. Have students create an epilogue panel (or panels) depicting an action, thought, resolution, or feeling that might occur if the story were to continue. Once the panels are completed, hang (or post) them for all to see. After they have been viewed, discuss and critique how they are similar or different and why. Discuss what seems to work best and why. Conversely, discuss what doesn't seem to work and why.

Taking These Basics Further

At this point you and your students are ready to explore, critically read, and discuss graphic novels. We encourage you to do so. The more you read and explore them on your own or together, the easier it will be to navigate and enjoy them. Recall that the Bonus Resource provides an extensive list of recommended graphic novels. You may want to begin there. Your local or school librarian may have additional suggestions.

To more fully understand how to read or to create graphic novels we strongly encourage you to explore Scott McCloud's two publications *Understanding Comics* and *Making Comics*. McCloud has been a pioneer in teaching others about the intricacies of reading and writing graphic novels. (McCloud's books are appropriate for grades 5+). For young readers, you may want to explore *Adventures in Cartooning* by James Sturm, or *How to Make Awesome Comics* by Neill Cameron. (Both of these resources are appropriate for grades 2 to 5.)

Selecting Appropriate Graphic Novels for Your Classroom

The best way to determine how appropriate a graphic novel selection is for your students is to take recommendations from lists or colleagues you trust, and then read your selections from cover to cover. You're the best judge of your students' reading level, your students' maturity level, and your school's and community's guidelines for appropriate reading materials. You are also the best equipped to recognize what will work best in your classroom. What many teachers still struggle with is figuring out where to find great kids' graphic novels.

One way to find them, as we mentioned earlier, is to ask your local and/or school librarian. Librarians are excellent resources for a number of reasons. First, they know your students and community. They also know which titles are popular among your students. If your favorite librarian is at a loss for appropriate recommendations, here are a few resources we've found extremely helpful:

- The American Library Association (ALA.org), including its Association for Library Service to Children (ALSC), is an excellent resource. Here's the ALA's latest (as of our publication date) information: "Graphic Novels Reading Lists – 2016 Update" at www .ala.org/alsc/graphicnovels2016

- The School Library Journal (www.slj.com) is another excellent resource that has ongoing reviews of kids' graphic novels.

- Please check this book's website periodically, as we'll be providing ongoing graphic novel reviews.

- The Comic Book Legal Defense Fund has an ongoing online column titled "Using Graphic Novels in Education." Each post highlights a particular graphic novel. It provides a summary or overview, suggested lesson and/or discussion ideas, suggested prose pairings, and additional online resources for content-area lessons. You can find these posts at cbldf.org/?s=using+graphic+novels+in+education.

Want more suggestions? The Bonus Resource for this book contains a list of kids' graphic novels we like, along with suggested reading and grade levels, a brief synopsis of each story, and important notes. Appendix B contains a few additional resources with reading lists.

5

MOTIVATION

Graphic novels are fantastic motivators. Research has shown that teachers using graphic novels report a noticeable increase in students' reading, participation, and engagement in the content found within graphic novels (as was discussed in greater detail in Chapter 2). The trick is that motivating students, like most skills, requires preparation and monitoring. Students need to be immediately engaged, and that engagement must be maintained and held as a unit progresses in its degree of challenge. Moreover, different people are motivated differently. Some students may think it's immensely cool that you're using a graphic novel, while others would rather read a chapter book.

The purpose of this chapter is to give you the tools to use graphic novels to help motivate a wider range of students in your classroom. We start by helping you assess your students' interests and motivations, primarily in the classroom, with an eye toward understanding the individuals in your class as students, as collaborators, and as friends. We then discuss different strategies to best engage your diverse students throughout a unit. Throughout, we address graphic novels' motivating power, the possible perils they may pose, and how to navigate both.

Getting to Know Your Students

The first step in assessing how to use graphic novels to motivate your students is to play detective. As a teacher, you probably already have a good sense of who your students are as classroom participants. For example, you probably know who will always have a hand raised after a question and who, like clockwork, will be talking with friends not five minutes into the lesson. Most of your observations, however, are probably informal. We'd like to present a more formal lens through which to collect and interpret your students' interests and affinities. We suggest that as you observe your students, you also take notes along the lines of the following questions. Note that we encourage you to make your observations not only in the classroom but also at recess, at lunch, and around the school.

1. Are your students comfortable taking risks? What do they see as "risky"?

2. Are your students artistic?

3. How much do your students socialize? With whom and when do they socialize? How well do they work with their friends?

4. What movies, books, TV shows, games, and the like do your students like to watch, read, or play in their free time? Do you notice any specific genres or topics that stand out as particularly popular?

From these observations, you can then build a profile of each student and of your class as a whole, allowing you to fine-tune your curricula. We continue by taking a closer look at each of these questions.

Are Your Students Comfortable Taking Risks?

Here are some things to keep in mind when considering this question:

- How creative do you find each student to be?

- How eager are your students to try something new? How strongly and frequently do they resist new things?

- What routines exist in your classroom? What happens when you break or switch up your routine?

- What happens when you ask each student to do things outside of his or her comfort zone? In what ways do students resist?

- Have students ever referred to themselves as "good" or "bad" at something? "Smart" or "stupid"? How do they self-identify and self-evaluate as students?

Recognizing the Importance of Creating and Breaking Routines

Students tend to become accustomed to class running in a certain way. They expect to read certain kinds of books, have a class discussion analyzing elements of the book, work on group activities, have homework assigned at the end of the day or period, and at the end of the unit, have some form of assessment, be it a test or quiz, essay, or project. You've possibly set the class routine to be somewhat predictable, as students will be less confused about what they need to do, thus reclaiming some valuable class time.

The problem is that when things become predictable, students learn when they can comfortably "tune out" certain parts of the class and when they need to refocus. A routine can make class less surprising and, as a result, less exciting. Graphic novels, whether students are reading them or creating them, can rock some of this routine as well as pleasantly surprise and intrigue your students, opening the door to further engagement.

Graphic novels break your routine. They don't look like textbooks, and you'll be asking students to think and do things (like looking at pictures) that they don't generally associate with classwork. On the one hand, for students who do not see themselves as "smart" in language arts and who frequently give up, graphic novels may be sufficiently different to empower them. For once, they may feel class approaching their "comfort" zone. On the other hand, you may be encouraging strong language learners to explore and take risks that further their language skills in surprising new ways. For all students, it will be a different type of classroom adventure.

We recommend leveraging the motivating power of graphic novels by giving students a lot of activities and questions that are different from what they normally do. Following is an activity we recommend for a number of reasons. First, for most of your classrooms it is a break from routine. It involves your students standing up, moving around, and thinking about poses they need to make. You can creatively explore student groups and grouping. Moreover, it is a great segue into how to read or write graphic novels, as it deals with understanding the importance of composing meaningful and evocative scenes. Finally, with origins dating back to the nineteenth century, it is an activity that can be extended beyond the graphic novel.

LESSON: THE TABLEAU VIVANT

Mastery Objective. Students will learn essential elements needed to create a dynamic and visually engaging scene.

Introducing the Lesson

Define the term *tableau*: A group of motionless figures who represent a scene, often from a story or from history (plural: *tableaux*).

Guided Practice

Ask for four volunteers. Have them go to the front of the classroom while you move off to the side.

Tell the four students that they will be presenting a scene in a tableau. You will give them a title for the tableau that they are to present; you will then count down from 3 and yell, "FREEZE!" (*Note* that you want to surprise the class with the title, so refrain from giving it until after students fully comprehend what they will need to do.)

Ask if students have any clarifying questions.

Give the volunteers the tableau title: "A Day at the Beach." Then slowly count down from 3, and yell, "FREEZE!" At this point, your volunteers should be frozen in their tableau.

Ask the class what worked well in the tableau: How clear is the scene being depicted? Is the scene interesting to look at? Is the scene dynamic? You will likely need to ask pointed questions to get to the following three guidelines for scenes:

a. Facial expressions. The actors need to show through their facial expressions how they feel about the events going on.

b. TMT (stands for "too much tushie"). In order for the audience to best see what's going on, the actors need to face the audience. If one actor needs to look at another actor in

(continued)

a scene (for example, if they're talking to each other), the best practice is generally to have each person angled so she or he is partially facing the other person and partially facing the audience.

c. Levels. To make a scene look interesting, make sure that some people are standing, some are seated, and others are leaning. This creates several levels and makes the scene look more dynamic.

List the guidelines "Facial expressions," "TMT," and "Levels" on the board during the conversation. Talk about how these three elements are important guidelines not only for constructing a tableau but also for composing a graphic novel panel, a scene for a play, or any other visual image.

Ask for a fifth volunteer for a second tableau. Tell this student that his or her role is a surprise because it's a little different. Instruct this student to stand next to you. When all the volunteers are ready, tell them: "After I give you the title of this tableau, I'll count down from 3 and have you freeze." Before continuing, make sure that your instructions are understood. Then introduce the new tableau: "Your tableau's title is 'A day at the beach BUT THERE'S A SHARK!'" Now, point to the fifth student to signify that he or she is the shark. Continue by counting down from 3, and yelling, "FREEZE!"

Open the conversation by asking all the students if anything needs to be adjusted given the three guidelines written on the board. Often, the levels guideline needs to be addressed, since the volunteers didn't have time to plan the scene as a group. Continue by asking what worked well in this tableau. Use the conversation to pivot toward a fourth guideline (which you'll write on the board): "Line of sight," meaning that the viewer's eye needs to be directed by a straight line toward or away from a focal point.

Lesson Debrief and Assessment

Debrief. Ask the students why they think learning about tableaux is important. Discuss the importance of composition, how we make scenes interesting, and why interesting scenes are important.

Assessment. Break the class into groups of three or four. Give every group a different scene from the book that they most recently finished or are currently reading – this is also a chance to review content from past classes. Give the groups about five minutes to plan their tableaux. Have each group share their tableau. After each group presents, ask students for questions and comments, and as necessary, have the group adjust its tableau. Evaluate your students' understanding of scenes from their tableaux and their discussion comments.

Tableaux are effective for a number of reasons. They get students on their feet and active. At the same time, each tableau is fairly controlled; students can neither talk nor move, making opportunities to act out very limited. Furthermore, there's a creative element that they normally don't have. Finally, they have to create and communicate by thinking about how their bodies are positioned. This is a type of thinking that they normally don't do outside of gym.

Getting kids excited about visual elements in a scene can translate into getting kids excited about writing scenes in a visual format. You can also present tableau images to students and ask them to write dialogue for each image, getting them engaged in the writing process and character development. Similarly, you can use the image in Figure 5.1, a page from *Pirate Penguin vs Ninja Chicken: Escape from Skull-Fragment Island*, by Ray Friesen, where the original dialogue has been whited out.

Note: Figure 5.1 can be found in a reproducible format on our websites (www.wiley.com/go/worthathousandwords, meryljaffe.com, and taliahurwich.com)

FIGURE 5.1 *Pirate Penguin vs Ninja Chicken: Escape from Skull-Fragment Island*, without dialogue
Source: Ray Friesen, *Pirate Penguin vs Ninja Chicken*, Vol. 2: *Escape from Skull-Fragment Island* (Marietta, GA: Top Shelf Productions, 2016), p. 16, top two rows.

Ask students to imagine and compose what they think Pirate Penguin and Ninja Chicken are saying, based on what they're doing, their facial expressions, and their reactions to each other. (For reference, the actual dialogue can be seen in Figure 5.2.) You can use an activity like this to preview an upcoming chapter in the graphic novel your class is reading, or as a stand-alone activity. Furthermore, to tie this activity more into the tableau activity, you can ask students to create a tableau of each panel and then ask them to speak the dialogue they think would belong in each panel.

FIGURE 5.2 *Pirate Penguin vs Ninja Chicken: Escape from Skull-Fragment Island,* with dialogue
Source: Ray Friesen, *Pirate Penguin vs Ninja Chicken,* Vol. 2: *Escape from Skull-Fragment Island* (Marietta, GA: Top Shelf Productions, 2016), p. 16, top two rows.

Whether or not you choose to do this particular exercise, you can make many different connections and activities based on the similarities that exist between the graphic novel panel and the tableau.

This is an unusual approach, to say the least. As teachers, you are no doubt accustomed to graphic organizers, but the visual elements in this type of brainstorming are much less intimidating for visual thinkers and weak language learners.

However, while engaging students in new and different activities is an important way to motivate and empower certain students, breaking routines is not without a few challenges. In the next section, we will discuss the issues that come with introducing innovative materials and activities into your classroom.

Recognizing and Addressing the Challenges of Risk Taking

A potential challenge is that students who have become accustomed to your routines might become stressed when you change them. Particularly when presented with something new and unusual where they're unfamiliar with the expectations and demands for success, some students might shut down. Students often learn to do well by learning what the teacher wants. Students don't just simply learn content – they learn to read *you*.

When you do something different in your classroom (including using graphic novels), you become less predictable. This requires students to take risks. All of a sudden, students are reading different kinds of books, doing different kinds of activities, and being evaluated on skills they don't generally bring to a language arts classroom. This levels the field for many students, but can be frightening. As a result, it's important to meet and address these fears head-on yet without diminishing the importance of taking risks.

Despite the challenges of risk taking, we cannot downplay its importance. While all risks must be calculated, thinking outside the box, attempting and learning skills outside our comfort zones, and learning how to learn from failure are skills that allow us to grow throughout life. Taking risks in the classroom with a teacher guiding them enables students to learn how to judge, maneuver, and manage risks – skills they'll lean on and appreciate. As educators, we know this. We know that it's good for our strong students (or any student) to learn how to overcome the fears and frustrations of risk taking. As a result, it's important that students get the message from you that everyone struggles at some point. They need to see that you expect them to put their best effort into the lesson, but you aren't disappointed in them when their best isn't perfect.

In the next section, we address one particular risk – one that is often raised when teaching graphic novels – that of creating and evaluating art.

Are Your Students Artistic?

Here are some things to keep in mind when considering this question:

- Who doodles and who draws? Are these creations abstract images, whole scenes, or just characters?

- In their daily (or weekly) routine, how frequently are students asked to create and evaluate art?

- When they look at an image, are they detail-oriented or do they comment on the work as a whole?

- What kinds of visual images do you notice them interacting with on a regular basis?

Using Art in Language Arts Classrooms

Aside from expanding definitions and expectations for what makes someone good in school, drawing and illustrating encourages students to make creative choices they aren't used to making. It expands the very definition of "composition" and "storytelling" through a visual medium. When creating their own drawings, comics, or graphic novels, students are given the opportunity to make their own important choices – like what color to use or what angles or perspectives to take when looking at a scene. These choices make the art of communication and storytelling more meaningful while empowering, engaging, and motivating students, students' perceptions, and students' decisions.

Recognizing the Challenge of Using Art

In and out of school, students recognize that their writing skills are a work in progress that can be improved through practice and others' help. This recognition however, may not be transferred to drawing or artistic skills. Most students (and some adults) think that people either do or don't have artistic ability. This, however, is not true. We all can be artists. Unfortunately, something happens somewhere between kindergarten and second grade where drawing is relegated to a supporting role in the classroom while artistic acumen is often critically evaluated by peers. But the truth is anyone can draw, and with our booming digital and media age, even those who feel they can't draw can rely on computer apps to help.

The problem is that self-perceptions, even when based on incorrect facts, have a significant impact on students' motivations and accomplishments. Students' self-identification as "artistic" or "not artistic" will either heighten or lessen their sense of risk when you ask them to communicate in a way you've never evaluated them on before. Students who see themselves as being artistic will immediately be drawn to possibilities and opportunities for showing off their talent and doing well. Students who don't think that they're good at drawing may think that they'll never be good at it. Worse yet, they might fear that a skill they don't have will lead to their getting a bad grade.

Addressing Student Reluctance

No doubt, addressing each student's individual fear and reluctance in a more private setting could go a long way to encourage students to take risks as artists. However, we have also found two specific approaches that can help create an environment open to risk taking in the larger classroom: teaching students how to respectfully critique artwork and teaching them that artistic creativity in graphic novels can extend beyond simply illustrating. In the following sections, we will deal with each tactic, providing sample lessons to help you foster such skills and attitudes in your classroom.

Teaching to Respectfully Critique

At the heart of introducing anything new or different lies the need to set up an environment where students can give and receive constructive criticism. Students will need explicit instructions on how they are expected to react to their peers' comments and work. The problem is that understanding how to transfer what they know about critiquing prose into critiquing art requires complex thinking and executive functioning; some students may need a bit more hand-holding than others to ensure that they understand how to respectfully give feedback to struggling artists.

Creating a classroom environment more attuned to respectful critique requires you to once again be a detective. Are the students who don't draw or doodle sensitive to receiving criticism? Are the "class artists" good at being respectful? Does your school have a fine arts program you might be able to lean on? Answering these questions will give you a clearer sense of what to monitor.

Think about how you expect students to behave as they're giving constructive criticism. You may have already given them instructions on how to behave respectfully when thinking about their peers' work. Try to predict what will be the hardest rules for the students to keep. Finally, you may want to model receiving and accepting criticism. The next activity will, we hope, place *you* in a position where you are taking risks and not producing "perfect" work. Simultaneously, it will ask students to interact with you in a respectful manner as you're taking risks, having them model constructive criticism.

LESSON: MINI-COMIC COMPOSITION

Note that while this is designed to be an all-ages lesson, younger students may not yet have learned how to give constructive criticism. As a result, be prepared to spend extra time, when necessary, to more fully explain how to constructively critique.

Mastery Objective. Students will understand how and why to give constructive criticism when creating mini-comics.

Introducing the Lesson

- Review with students the elements that make up a graphic novel (frame, panel, dialogue, etc.).

- Ask students what constructive criticism means, and what they need to keep in mind when giving constructive criticism. If you don't already have a written list of ways to behave respectfully when giving feedback, write the list to the side of your board, leaving enough room for the activity itself.

Guided Practice

Tell students that the whole class will be creating a panel for a graphic novel re-telling of *Little Red Riding Hood*, specifically depicting the scene when Little Red Riding Hood first sees the wolf in the forest. Continue to instruct the students that while you will be drawing the actual panel, you will be relying upon the class's directions.

(continued)

Depending on the class, you may want to use guided questions such as these:

- Okay. So how do we want to draw Little Red Riding Hood?

- How do we show that she's feeling [a particular emotion]?

- What should be in the background?

- Do we want our characters saying anything?

At a certain point, start to ask, "Did we forget anything we should include in the panel?" This provides an opportunity for students to review what elements are required in a graphic novel panel.

As students are providing input, you should be drawing quickly – more sketching than actually illustrating, so mistakes will be made. Be lighthearted about mistakes and don't spend more than a second or two fixing anything. For example, Talia likes to joke with her students throughout this activity about how much her Big Bad Wolf looks like a Big Bad Squirrel. Be mindful of the students' comments, and if they are starting to give unconstructive criticism, pause the lesson and have students reflect on what they're saying and on how to realign their behavior.

Lesson Debrief and Assessment

Debrief. When you're finished with the panel, discuss with students why you did this exercise with *you* as the artist. Have students evaluate the way they gave you feedback as well as the way you took their feedback. Make sure that you return to the list of how to behave when giving or receiving critique. Ask students when it was most difficult to follow that list of rules, and what they did to try to be as respectful as possible.

Assessment. Have students break into groups of four and have them recreate – in a graphic novel panel – a scene from a book they have recently completed or are currently reading. Tell them that instead of evaluating them for the comic itself, you'll be evaluating them based on how they interact as a group. As they're working, make sure to circulate so you can assess how they're collaborating and giving feedback in an appropriate manner.

Teaching the Many Roles of Artists

Sometimes students can prove to be their own harshest critics. If you have a large number of students who are unmotivated specifically because of the visual elements in graphic novel lessons, you can use computer, tablet, or online apps to circumvent the need to illustrate (see Appendix B for a list of several apps and websites that can help you and your students to create comic strips and graphic novels). However, we also encourage you to emphasize that artists aren't just illustrators. Artists can be colorists or graphic designers or can engage in other modes of visual expression. Here we provide a sample lesson on one such mode – page design and layout.

LESSON: BECOMING A LAYOUT ARTIST

Mastery Objective. Have students learn and put into practice different ways a graphic novel page can be laid out.

Materials

- An envelope with panels cut from a few pages of a graphic novel.
- Scissors.
- Glue.
- Several pieces of white, legal-size printer paper.

Introducing the Lesson

- Tell students that in groups of four, they will be receiving panels from a graphic novel and will have to decide how to lay the panels out over a few pages. Ask the class what decisions they will have to make when trying to decide what goes where. Here are some possible ideas:

  - How "busy" should each page be? The more panels there are on a page, the less time readers will spend focusing on each panel.
  - Do they want to keep people from knowing what is going to happen on the next page?
  - How large should the gutters be between panels?
  - How many pages do they think the action should be spread over?
  - How large should the pages be? Students could, if they'd like, trim the legal-size paper to fit their panels. Furthermore, tell the students that the paper you gave them is larger than the pages in the original graphic novel, so they should feel comfortable keeping their pages legal-size, folding them in half to make very small pages, or trimming them to whatever size they think the original book was.

- Students may have other ideas. Write all ideas on the chalkboard, and leave the list up when the students break out into groups.

Independent Practice

Have students work with their groups on page layout for about 10 minutes. Ask students to present their page layouts at the end of that time, sharing what choices they made, and why they made them.

(continued)

Lesson Debrief and Assessment

Critique with students what was different and what was similar in the different groups' layouts. Ask students what about this activity was easy and what was difficult. Was there anything about this activity that surprised them? Return to the list of choices you made at first, and ask students if there are any additional choices they had to make that are not listed on the board. If there are, write them down. Ultimately, discuss how determining a page's layout is a creative process, and why it's so important.

Leveraging Collaboration and Group Work

Here are some things to keep in mind when considering how social your students are in a classroom environment:

- When given a choice, whom do students choose to work with and how productive is that work? How do they react when they are assigned to groups? When they are assigned seating?

- Who in your classroom is excited by group work, and who prefers to work alone?

- Whom do your students hang out with? Are those kids the same students who are in your classroom, or are they from elsewhere?

- Do your students ever try to whisper to friends during class? How do they respond when others whisper to them during class?

By incorporating various forms of communication (i.e. text, image, design), graphic novels provide great opportunities for collaboration. For example, comic books are frequently not written by a single person, but reflect a collaboration among a writer, an illustrator, a colorist, and an inker. Margaret Atwood, author of *The Handmaid's Tale* and a highly successful poet, novelist, and literary critic, has beautifully explained how important collaboration was when she created her first young adult graphic novel, *Angel Catbird*:

> I realized that Angel Catbird would have to look better than the flying cats I'd drawn. . . . So I would need a coauthor. But how to find one? . . . Then up on my Twitter feed popped, one day, a possible answer . . . and connected me not only with artist Johnnie Christmas, who could draw just the right kinds of muscles and also owl claws, but the publisher, Dark Horse Comics. The Dark Horse editor of the series is Daniel Chabon, who from his picture looks about fifteen. I have never met him, nor have I met Johnnie, nor the excellent colourist Tamra Bonvillain. . . .
>
> All of these collaborators have been wonderful. . . . Watching Angel Catbird come to life has been hugely engaging. There was, for instance, a long email debate about Angel's pants. He had to have pants of some kind. Feather pants, or what? And if feathers, what kind of feathers? And should these pants be underneath his human pants, and just sort of emerge? How should they manifest themselves? Questions would be asked, and we needed to have answers.
>
> **Margaret Atwood, Introduction to *Angel Catbird*, Vol. 1.**

By giving certain students "jobs," such as lead writer, lead artist, chief editor, panel and page designer, and so on, you can provide extra structure in group work while engaging students in communication and storytelling.

Another method of structuring group work around graphic novels is having students collaborate when critically reading a graphic novel. When discussing or evaluating a graphic novel, assign group members different responsibilities. For example, one student may critique the use of color, another the page design, another the choice of text, and so on.

Leveraging Student Affinities

Here are some question to keep in mind when considering what movies, books, TV shows, games, and the like your students like to watch, read, or play in their free time:

- What genres do your students like?

- Do they like happy stories? Sad stories? Dark stories?

- In relation to their age level, do they consume media that are more childish, or more mature?

While we like to devote much of our class time to the "classics" (and we both believe that you *should* – classic became classic for a reason), texts and media generally attributed to popular culture can be immensely motivating. Because these types of stories are also consumed outside of school, students can see how what they're learning in school can enrich their lives outside of school. Incorporating student affinities and passions, can also make your content area more inviting and more meaningful to them. Moreover, there are often valuable reading lessons to be found in popular culture. Please see the Bonus Resource for suggestions (and brief synopses) that will help you find relevant, appropriate texts that reflect your students' affinities.

In the following sample lesson, we ask students to reflect on their interests and affinities that would lead them into independent reading activity. As the lesson is presently written, we ask students to recommend graphic novels to their peers – an idea that could work with some classes, while students in other classes may not be able to empathize with other students enough to make recommendations based on their peers' tastes (instead of simply their own). In those situations, because the ultimate goal is for students to be self-reflective (and not necessarily be able to recommend books to friends), we suggest that you recommend graphic novels to students. Furthermore, it is important to note that this activity is dependent on the availability of a diverse graphic novel collection at your school or local library. Before running this lesson, check in with your local or school librarian to see whether the breadth of the library's graphic novel collection can support this activity.

LESSON: FINDING A GOOD GRAPHIC NOVEL

Mastery Objective. Students will have a deeper understanding of what kinds of stories they enjoy and be more reflective when selecting books.

Materials Needed

Magazine pages, images, or materials that can be used for students to create collages. Conversely, if students have access to computers to create a collage using online images and word art, you may consider using those digital tools instead.

Introducing the Lesson

Talk with the students about how they choose the books they read, the television they watch, the games they play, the after-school activities they do, and the movies they watch. Did they ever choose a move, book, or show that they ultimately didn't like? Tell students that this lesson is about learning to make recommendations to friends as well as strategies for choosing new books to read and movies and shows to watch.

Guided Practice

Have students jot down on scratch paper their two most favorite books, two most favorite television shows, two most favorite movies, and at least three sports, games, or after-school activities or hobbies that they enjoy doing in their free time.

Ask students to share any patterns they see when thinking about all the things they enjoy.

Independent Practice

Students should make a collage of the things they like to do, play, watch, and/or read. The collage should include the books, films, TV shows, and activities they listed during the guided practice as well as other information about things they generally like to read, watch, and do. If students are making these collages on the computer (and can control the size of the words and images), recommend that they make the titles and activities they like the most larger than other titles and activities. Add that these collages are going to be used to help their peers select graphic novel recommendations, so the more detailed the information they include, the more likely it is that their peers will be able to find something they'll really enjoy.

When students are finished, distribute the collages so each student has someone else's collage. Then, using resources such as your school library, local librarian, and/or trusted reviews and book lists such as those from the *School Library Journal* (www.slj.com) and the American Library Association (www.ala.org/yalsa/great-graphic-novels), students should make a list recommending at least three graphic novels to the classmate whose collage they have, including a brief paragraph explaining why they are recommending each graphic novel. This list of recommendations should be passed to the collage's creator.

Lesson Debrief and Assessment

Debrief. Ask students what strategies they used to find recommendations for their classmates. Did they learn any new strategies in finding books to read? Record students' strategies for finding books on the board, and have students copy these strategies in their notes. At the end, feel free to include any extra pointers and recommendations of your own, so students will have a resource they can use in the future when selecting new books (or movies, TV shows, etc.) for themselves.

Assessment. Each student should pick one book from their list of recommendations, read it, and write a book report about it. The book report should include two sections:

- Toward the beginning, students should write why they chose that particular graphic novel out of the three recommendations. What in their collage made this particular graphic novel the most appealing (or the least unappealing)?

- At the end, they should write, based on having now read the book, what they would do to amend the collage they made during the independent practice. What would they add? What might they take out?

USING GRAPHIC NOVELS TO TEACH READING

Appealing to both visual and verbal learners, graphic novels look and feel simple and unimposing. Ironically though, behind graphic novels' deceptive simplicity lie complex texts, making them ideal for reading instruction. From their highlighted sound effects and advanced vocabulary to their succinct and often playful use of language and their engaging characters, stories, and images, graphic novels are powerful language learning tools.

While there are clear benefits to incorporating these texts into your reading instruction, there are lurking challenges you may initially face as well. In this chapter, we first address these challenges and then present examples of how to use graphic novels when teaching reading and reading comprehension.

Addressing the Challenges of Integrating Graphic Novels into Your Reading Curriculum

One of the challenges teachers not familiar with graphic novels may have is finding and determining appropriate anchor and instructional texts. Another challenge may arise in getting students to slow down when reading them. For many students and teachers, such slowing down seems counterintuitive. However, for comprehension, readers must often slow down their reading (especially when relatively new to this format) as they learn how to incorporate vital details and pertinent information found in the illustrations, design, and text. This can be particularly challenging for middle-level readers who are beginning to speed up their prose reading. Let's take a closer look at these challenges, and at the solutions we've found helpful.

Finding Appropriate Graphic Novel Texts

One reason selecting appropriate graphic novels for reading instruction may be challenging is that determining a graphic novel's reading level using traditional measures doesn't always work. Traditional measures look at word count, vocabulary, and sentence structure. While word count is significantly lower in graphic novels (distorting the reading level downward), the vocabulary and sentence structure can be quite complex (skewing the reading level upward). This, however, isn't necessarily a bad thing. Graphic novels' concise text, sophisticated vocabulary, and often-complex sentence structure, make them motivating teaching tools for your students' diverse needs and skill levels.

When considering graphic novels as instructional and/or anchor texts, we strongly recommend consulting with your school librarian and colleagues. No need to reinvent the wheel if you don't have to. They may know which graphic novels your students are reading independently, helping you to determine appropriate instructional level texts.

If your librarian and colleagues are not familiar with specific graphic novels, we recommend that you keep the mnemonic CRAVE in mind. This means that when selecting an appropriate text, you will consider **C**ontent and theme, **R**eadability and language use, **A**ttention to details, **V**ocabulary, and **E**xternal resources.

- **C**ontent and theme

  - Are the plot, genre, and writing or illustration style teachable, engaging, appropriate, and accessible for your students?

  - Does the selection meet your students' interests and their (reading and cognitive) instructional level skills?

  - Does the content (theme, art, language) make this selection appropriate as an anchor or instructional text, as an independent reading text, or as a motivational text?

  - What about this particular book directly addresses your instructional goals? (For example, is it a particularly strong choice for teaching onomatopoeia, for teaching metaphor and simile, or for teaching close reading?)

  - Does the addition of this text add to and/or support themes found in other texts your students study during the year?

- **R**eadability and language use: Do the book's grammatical structure, sentence complexity, and visual and verbal literary devices meet instructional needs?

- **A**ttention to details: Are the details (illustration details and design) manageable for your students' attention and comprehension skills?

- **V**ocabulary: Is the content (i.e. vocabulary, theme, art) appropriate for your students?

- **E**xternal resources: Use the resources we provide in this chapter and in Appendix B and the online Bonus Resource, and also consult colleagues for suggestions, guides, and/or syllabi you can adapt and use.

Recall that in the Bonus Resource, we list and describe our favorite graphic novels, including content and themes and also ages and grade levels. In Appendix A we list resources to help you support your selection choices. In Appendix B we provide resources with additional support for selecting graphic novels as well as resources for finding, using, and making them. Furthermore, another way to check the age appropriateness of a particular book is to enter the book title in the search bar on the Common Sense Media website (www.commonsensemedia.org).

Finally, keep in mind that throughout this book, we use and introduce images and teaching suggestions from a variety of graphic novels that we've vetted. In this chapter, you'll sample anchor texts for teaching phonics, language use and literary devices, comprehension (theme, character, and story and plot development), and critical and close reading. But first we address one other challenge you may find: training students to slow down while monitoring comprehension.

Training Readers to Slow Down

Training readers to slow down when reading graphic novels, in order to attend to details, is essential when teaching reading with graphic novels. This can be a challenge for your stronger readers who are used to quickly swimming through the text, and for students with weak attention skills. The first thing you'll need to do is have your students recognize that they need to slow down for comprehension as they integrate graphic novels' various storytelling elements.

To help your kids remember and incorporate this challenge, the following mnemonic device may help:

THINK . . . OREO – super stuffed with story fun!

Observe details in the text, panel images, and design elements.

Read text provided in dialogue, thought, and narrative balloons.

Evaluate what you just read or saw in and between the panels to make sure it makes sense before continuing.

Onward to the next panel or page.

After introducing this mnemonic, we suggest using the sample lesson given here, with one of three possible anchor texts (one for younger, one for middle, and one for older students), to help train your students and/or reinforce their ability to slow down and attend to details.

LESSON: SEARCH, DISCOVER, AND ATTEND TO DETAILS

Mastery Objective. Students will understand how and why it's important to slow down and attend to details when reading (especially with graphic novels).

Materials Needed

- One (or all) of the Search and Discover images shown in Figures 6.1, 6.2, and/or 6.3, or images from any other graphic novel page that has a lot going on.

FIGURE 6.1 *Space Dumplins* search and discover
Source: Craig Thompson, *Space Dumplins* (New York: Scholastic, 2015), p. 4.

Note: Each of these figures (6.1, 6.2, and 6.3) and their Search and Discover objects can be found in a reproducible format on our websites (www.wiley.com/go/worthathousand-words, meryljaffe.com, and taliahurwich.com)

Search and discover *Space Dumplins*: a floating barge (ship); half-eaten platforms; the alphabet; student desks; a broken, floating metal scaffold; floating computers; floating engines, some gushing ooze; floating screw; floating bolt; an air freshener; a computer screen; floating book; floating scroll of paper; confusion; concern; love; celebration; crazy text with "MY SCHOOL!"; and the school's name (at least part of it).

Search and discover *Xoc: The Journey of a Great White*: jellyfish; aluminum soda cans; sea-weed; spoon; plastic bags; hammer; bottle; milk carton (pint); saucepan; baseball; piece of

FIGURE 6.2 *Xoc: The Journey of a Great White* search and discover
Source: Matt Dembicki, *Xoc: The Journey of a Great White* (Portland, OR: ONI Press, 2012), pp. 58–59.

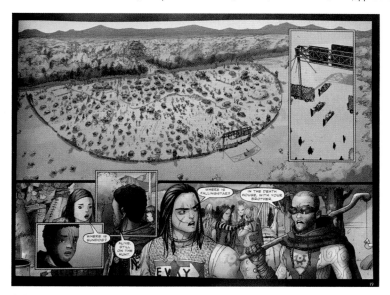

FIGURE 6.3 *Tribes: The Dog Years* search and discover
Source: Michael Geszel, Peter Spinetta, and Inaki Miranda, *Tribes: The Dog Years* (San Diego, CA: IDW, 2010), p. 19.

(continued)

driftwood; empty can opened by a can opener; stop sign; pipes; sock; chair; button-down shirt; wheel; shovel; book; ladder; fear; confusion; hunger; symbiotic relationships.

Search and discover *Tribes: The Dog Years*: sleds; highway posts and signs; tattoo #1; tattoo #2; tattoo #3; tattoo #4; Death House; One-Way sign; New York Yankees shirt; a rubber duckie; goggles; fence on wheels; a watch tower; time of day; time of year; where on Earth this may be; fear; concern; reunions.

- Copies of the Search and Discover Worksheet for students to fill in, noting specific items they found in the text's images, where they found them, and what they think each item might be telling us about the characters, plot, and themes of the story.

Search and Discover Worksheet

Directions. As you find items in the graphic novel image please record the item found;

- where you found it – giving the panel number and where in the panel we can find it; and

- what you think the item, sound, symbol, or emotion means and what it tells us about the setting, the characters, and the plot.

Search and Discover Worksheet

Student Name _____

Item found	Where I found it (panel # and where it is in the panel)	What it tells me about the setting, characters, and plot

_____

_____

_____

_____

_____

_____

_____

_____

_____

_____

_____

_____

_____

_____

_____

Introducing the Lesson

▫ Tell students that you will be beginning a unit using graphic novels, but before proceeding, they will need to learn how to slow down to appreciate and integrate all the details they'll find in the text, the images, and the panel and page designs.

▫ Review the mnemonic OREO, and what students will need to keep in mind when reading graphic novels (you may want to review Chapter 4 for more details).

▫ Introduce the following guided practice activity, where students will be going on a "search and rescue" mission and attempting to find lost items in the selected anchor text.

Guided Practice (a whole class activity)

Direct students to search and find various elements and details embedded in the image from the anchor text they are using – as spelled out in the list that follows each image (Figure 6.1, 6.2, or 6.3).

With the whole class, search for one or two of the items, leaving the remaining items for your students to find on their own (as detailed in the independent practice to follow).

The point here is for your students to realize that there is so much information to take in from the text and images that if they don't slow down and carefully examine the given text, image, and design, they may very well miss important details.

(continued)

Once you've all searched and found a few of the items, discuss these points:

- How hard or easy it was to find them.
- Why (in the students' opinion) the author(s) included them.
- What these elements tell us about the character(s) or story.

Finally, introduce the Search and Discover Worksheet, which students will use to continue to search for objects, actions, and reactions. Before students work on their own, make sure they have written down the items listed in the search and discover paragraph that follows the figure they're using, putting the items into the first column of their worksheet. Then instruct students to fill in the other columns as they consider what piece of the story each object, action, and reaction tells us. You may want to fill in the first row or two together, to make sure they understand the exercise.

Independent Practice

Direct students to continue examining the image on their own while they complete the worksheet.

Once they're done, meet as a group to discuss what they found and what they think the items found tell them about the plot, characters, setting, and so forth.

Lesson Debrief and Assessment

Discuss where each of the objects, emotions, actions, and reactions is to be found, what you all think each one means, and how it helps tell the story. Make sure to point out that in making sense of a page, reading the text alone or looking at the images alone doesn't really help with deciphering the story line. Readers clearly need to piece *all* the pieces together. Evaluate the worksheets completed by your students.

Once students are comfortable slowing down and attending to the visual and verbal data in front of them, you're ready to move on to incorporating graphic novels as anchor and/or instructional texts for reading (or any other) instruction.

Note that if you find they're not quite ready to move on, you may want to have them read graphic novels with no text, such as *Korgi* or *Owly*. (See the Bonus Resource for details.)

Using Graphic Novels for Reading Instruction

In the remainder of this chapter, we demonstrate how graphic novels can be used as anchor and instructional texts for teaching phonics, language use, comprehension and close or critical reading, literary devices (such as onomatopoeia, hyperbole, alliteration, simile, and metaphor), and plot and character development.

Phonics and Onomatopoeia

For young and emerging English language learners who are exploring phonics and letter sounds, graphic novels are motivating and instructive. They are full of inviting fonts and bizarrely highlighted words. In addition to highlighting specific sight words, they visually and verbally play with phonics, word sounds, and sound effects as fun-sounding words are splashed and highlighted across their pages. Just look at Figure 6.4, a page taken from *Sparks*, by Ian Boothby and Nina Matsumoto.

FIGURE 6.4 Text effects in *Sparks*.
Source: Ian Boothby and Nina Matsumoto, *Sparks* (New York: Scholastic, 2018), p. 28.

Not all graphic novels, however, have onomatopoeia and sound effects splashed across their pages. There are many graphic novels, like *Zita the Spacegirl* by Ben Hatke, as seen in Figure 6.5, that have sections with detailed images and limited or no text.

Looking at these two very different graphic novel page spreads, we hope to demonstrate some of graphic novels' versatility that allows teachers to use their pages in various instructional ways when teaching early reading and phonics and sight vocabulary instruction.

For example, after pointing out how graphic novels like *Sparks* use phonics and onomatopoeia, you might create a list of school scenes or scenarios with your students. Then in groups, as a class, or individually, students can create their own comic strip based on the scenarios brainstormed, and have fun inserting their own sound effects and onomatopoeia.

Or you may take any given graphic novel page and white out the various text balloons. Then have students create their own dialogue or sound effects. If you have students do this individually

FIGURE 6.5 Limited use of text in *Zita the Spacegirl*
Source: Ben Hatke, *Zita the Spacegirl* (New York: First Second, 2011), p. 19.

or in groups, it is always fascinating fun to see the different text variations students generate from the same images.

Here are some anchor and instructional texts you may want to explore for highlighting word and letter sounds, sound effects, and onomatopoeia.

Grades 1–3

- *The Misadventures of Salem Hyde: Spelling Trouble*, by Frank Cammuso
- *Hilo: The Boy Who Crashed to Earth*, by Judd Winick
- *Dog Man* (series), by Dav Pilky

Grades 2–5

- *Mal and Chad* (series), by Stephen McCranie
- *Dream Jumper* (series), by Greg Grunberg and Lucas Turnbloom
- *Giants Beware!* (series), by Rafael Rosado and Jorge Aguirre
- *Hilo: The Boy Who Crashed to Earth*, by Judd Winick
- *Babymouse* (series), by Jennifer Holm and Matthew Holm
- *Squish* (series), by Jennifer Holm and Matthew Holm
- *Red's Planet* (series), by Eddie Pittman

Grades 4–7

- *Ghosts*, by Raina Telgemeier
- *Beanworld* (series), by Larry Marder
- *The Whole World's Crazy* (*Amelia Rules!* series), by Jimmy Gownley
- *Amulet: The Stone Keeper*, by Kazu Kibuishi
- *Monster on the Hill*, by Rob Harrell
- *Roller Girl*, by Victoria Jamieson

Grades 5+

- *LumberJanes: Beware the Kitten Holy*, by Noelle Stevenson, Grace Ellis, Shannon Watters, and Brooke Allen
- *Nimona*, by Noelle Stevenson
- *The Olympians* (series), by George O'Connor

Wordplay, Language Usage, and Vocabulary

We all use words all the time, often overlooking the power of their immediate and long-term effects. While many readers turn to graphic novels for their images and art, they are also excellent resources for relaying the power of words and wordplay.

Here are some examples of anchor and instructional texts that can be used to teach, reinforce, and highlight vocabulary, puns, and dynamic wordplay.

The Misadventures of Salem Hyde: Spelling Trouble, by Frank Cammuso (grades 1–3), is about a young witch who has problems spelling: her spells bizarrely backfire. The title gives only a hint of the wordplay (and homophones) readers will explore.

Hilo, by Judd Winick (series; grades 2–7). Throughout this series, there's wonderful wordplay as Hilo learns English and inadvertently discovers knock-knock jokes.

Babymouse, by Jennifer Holm and Matthew Holm (series; grades 2–5). One of Babymouse's endearing qualities (along with her vivid imagination) is her tendency to exaggerate. As a result, the series is rife with hyperbole (as well as metaphors, puns, and idioms). Figure 6.6 illustrates one of the many examples of how books in this series use wordplay.

Amelia Rules! by Jimmy Gownley (series; grades 4–7). This series is full of wordplay including onomatopoeia, acronyms, and insults, and the character Reggie's tendency to create words (such as "Sneezicus Barfona" for the Common Sneeze Barf, and "Hangtavious Outacus" for Hanging Out).

Nathan Hale's Hazardous Tales, by Nathan Hale (series; grades 4–8), depicts events from American history with fun facts, humor, puns, and wordplay. Here is one example, from the tale called *One Dead Spy* (p. 71): "Killed by lightning. How horrible." "Shocking."

Beanworld, by Larry Marder (series; grades 4–7), is part adventure, part a journey into the meaning of life and family, and all wonderful fun. There is wordplay from the title of the first book, "Wahoolazuma!" to the names of the characters (Mr. Spook, Professor Garbanzo, and Beanish – to name just a few), to the author's Chow Band songs, to his tweaking of familiar and newly coined words. This book will have readers thinking about and savoring words, songs, and more, and is a classroom gem when it comes to wordplay.

The Gettysburg Address, by Jonathan Hennessey (grades 5+), looks at Lincoln's Gettysburg Address and the power and intent of its words and phrases.

Reading Comprehension and Close Reading

With graphic novels, reading between the lines takes on a literal as well as figurative meaning. Their nature and their design lend themselves as tools for strengthening inference making and comprehension skills.

While reading comprehension refers to the ability to read and understand a given text, it involves much more than decoding. It involves

FIGURE 6.6 Wordplay in *Babymouse: Dragonslayer*
Source: Jennifer Holm and Matthew Holm, *Babymouse: Dragonslayer* (New York: Random House, 2009), p. 62.

- recognizing and understanding vocabulary and establishing a comfort level with navigating the given sentence structure;

- recognizing and ordering story elements (that are not always given sequentially);

- making inferences – hypothesizing and filling in story elements not given (or not initially given) – and being flexible enough to tweak one's understanding when necessary;

- integrating information given in the text with one's own understanding of people, cultures, and the world around us;

- recognizing author and character intents; and

- being motivated to continue to read and engage in the given text.

Recognizing and Understanding Text

We've already discussed how graphic novels' use of wordplay and fun with phonics can be used to develop and expand students' vocabulary and their comfort with reading in and out of classrooms. The more comfortable students are with text, the more prepared they are to navigate various text formats and text complexities.

Ordering Story Elements

Graphic novels' design and their sequential presentation of a story in discrete panels help students become more aware of recognizing and ordering story elements. Furthermore, page and panel designs and arrangements across and down the pages allow readers to "see" and integrate the ordering of critical and not-so-critical story events. Teachers can copy comic pages, break, or cut up the individual panels, and have students explore the effect of different panel arrangements and sequences of events.

Making Inferences

Graphic novels encourage and reinforce inference making and critical thinking in a number of ways. First, readers are constantly making, testing, and tweaking inferences as they fill in the gaps between panels. Teaching students to pause between panels to evaluate and then fill in what's missing helps students to slow down, to be more mindful of what is given and what is missing, and to cognitively construct story and character elements.

In addition to filling in gutter gaps between panels, readers also have to evaluate and construct social and emotional elements of character and story that are implied in images and text. While in prose texts this information is typically provided in narrative or dialogue, in graphic novels these elements are typically presented in the images. The images show facial expressions and body language. They also play with distance between characters, forcing readers to infer characters' feelings and reactions. Color and text font size and shape can also relay emotion and reactions. An added benefit of graphic novels is that because readers *see* and then fill in characters' emotions and reactions (from body language), it becomes much easier for students to be more aware of real-life social cues. As these social cues are given both visually and verbally, they are more concrete and can be more effectively dissected. Furthermore, students can learn to dissect these cues at their own pace, returning to relevant images and pages on their own and as often as needed, until the lessons they offer are incorporated.

For example, in Figure 6.7, taken from *American Born Chinese* by Gene Luen Yang, we see Jin Wang at his first day in his new school. Reading Yang's narrative at the top of the page, we realize Jin Wang (the young Chinese boy at the front of the class) is narrating what's happening:

> On the morning after we arrived, with the scent of our old home still lingering on my clothes, I was sent off to Mrs. Greeder's Third Grade at Mayflower Elementary School.

Notice how rich in detail this first sentence is. Then there's a play with the homophones "scent" and "sent" ("with the scent of our old home still lingering on my clothes . . . I was

FIGURE 6.7 Social cues in *American Born Chinese*
Source: Gene Luen Yang, *American Born Chinese* (New York: First Second, 2006), p. 30.

sent . . ."). We learn right away that Jin feels helpless. It wasn't his choice to leave his old home, nor was it his choice to be in this new school (he was sent).

Looking at Yang's images, we see so much more of the story. First, we see the teacher. She's smiling, wearing bright shiny star earrings. We infer that she's enthusiastic and well meaning (she has her hand gently resting on Jin's shoulder), but she's clueless (her eyes are always closed). Then there is Jin, who clearly isn't happy to be there, and as quietly as possible (so as to show respect and not embarrass his teacher), he gently tries to correct her mistakes (with his name and where he's from). Finally, look at the students' reactions. One girl seems surprised, the boy next to her hostile, one seems curious (as he's leaning over to see from behind the girl in front of him), while many of the others don't seem to care at all. It's no wonder Jin doesn't want to be there. And all of this is told through their expressions and body language.

Learning to read social cues through text and body language and image aids reading comprehension and helps us all learn to function more effectively socially. Dissecting social cues found in text and image is much akin to close reading of complex texts, a tool also used to aid reading comprehension.

Close Reading

Close reading involves examining difficult, complex texts. It's a skill that when mastered, empowers all learners to better navigate a greater variety of texts. When teaching close reading, we ask students to read and reread texts as they discover layers of meaning. With subsequent readings students uncover more and more answers to these questions:

- What does the text say?
- How does it say it?
- What does the content mean?
- What was the author's intent?
- How does the content inspire us?

Students, however, tend to resist close-reading instruction, and increasing their motivation and strengthening their extended attention are often instructional challenges. Graphic novels can help. They tend to lend themselves naturally to close reading because their story components are inherently deconstructed. Analyzing their layers feels meaningful and is engaging for diverse student learners. (You may want to reflect for a moment on your attention and interest levels in Chapters 3 and 4 as we modeled close reading of *March*.)

Let's take a look at what a close reading of a graphic novel may look like. In the following close reading lesson, we demonstrate this, using *Soupy Leaves Home*, by Cecil Castellucci and Jose Pimienta. This book is geared for grades 5+. For younger readers, you may want to use *The Misadventures of Salem Hyde: Spelling Trouble*, by Frank Cammuso (use page 1 for introducing the lesson and page 64 for independent student work).

LESSON: CLOSE READING *SOUPY LEAVES HOME* FOR DEEPER COMPREHENSION (GRADES 5+)

Mastery Objective. Students will close (critically) read a graphic novel page by analyzing its content (the author's text, image, and design choices), its perspectives, and the characters' and author's intents.

Materials Needed

- An anchor text from a graphic novel. This lesson will work with any graphic novel of your choice.
- Close Reading with Graphic Novels Rubric. *Note* that you may want to provide two blank copies of the rubric to each student. One to use for the guided practice and one to use for independent practice.

Note: This Close Reading with Graphic Novels Rubric can be found in a reproducible format on our websites (www.wiley.com/go/worthathousandwords, meryljaffe.com, and taliahurwich.com)

Close Reading with Graphic Novels Rubric

Student Name _____

Phase 1: Surface level	Phase 2: Structure – what the author is showing us: Analyze the vocabulary, font, image, page and panel design, angle, and/or perspective.	Phase 3: Deeper meaning – what the author means to tell us: Analyze the author's choices in text, image, and design (why the panel/page looks the way it does), and how these choices help us understand the story.	Phase 4: Inspiration – what we can learn from this: Analyze what we can guess or infer about the characters and their thoughts and actions, and what we can learn about our own lives from this.
What is taking place, and where and when this is happening:			
What the characters are doing:			
What the characters are thinking:			
What the characters are saying:			
What the characters are feeling:			
What the main idea is:			
Evidence telling us it's the main idea:			
What the supporting details are:			
Why these supporting details are important:			

Rubric Directions

This rubric lays out close reading in four phases. Each phase is represented in a column.

As you read the graphic novel, and notice the following details, write them down in the first column: Phase 1: Surface level.

- What is taking place, and where and when this is happening.
- What the characters are doing.
- What the characters are thinking.
- What the characters are saying.

(continued)

- What the characters are feeling.
- What the main idea is.
- Evidence telling us it's the main idea.
- What the supporting details are.
- Why these supporting details are important.

Then, for each detail filled in for Phase 1, move across the row as you analyze structure, deeper meaning, and inspiration:

- Phase 2: Structure – analyze what the author is showing us with the words, font, image, page and panel design, angle, and/or perspective.

- Phase 3: Deeper meaning – analyze what the author means to tell us through choices of text, image, and design, evaluating why the panel or page looks the way it does, and how these choices help us understand the story.

- Phase 4: Inspiration – analyze what we can learn, guess, or infer about the characters and their thoughts and actions, and what we can learn about our own lives from this.

Introducing the Lesson

- *Introduce and/or review close reading steps* readers should use to understand complex texts. Discuss how, when trying to understand any given text, readers have to read and reread a text (especially a complex one) to best understand the words and also the characters' and even the author's intent. (*Note* that we've broken close reading down into four phases. Feel free to tweak this exercise for your own class or lesson needs and objectives.)

- You may want to select a short, complex autobiographical or nonfiction text to demonstrate. Ask students what they think of this process. What they like and don't like about it. What is easy and what is hard. Next, tell them that they're going to try close reading text with a twist – by using graphic novels.

- *Introduce your text.* In our sample lesson, we use *Soupy Leaves Home*, by Cecil Castellucci and Jose Pimienta – a story about Pearl ("Soupy"), who runs away from home (for reasons revealed later) and then joins a hobo in trekking across the country. Pearl just can't find "warmth" in her formally loving home, no matter how hard she tries. In the initial pages, we see Pearl walking out of her house during the day. After passing through the town, she arrives at the railroad station. It is now night. At this point, we get a better look at Pearl. We see she's got a black eye; we see her waiting for and then riding the train in the dark of night. We then see her stealing clothes, cutting her hair, and trying to look like a boy. We're told this is the story of how she became warm again.

Guided Practice

Introduce the Close Reading with Graphic Novels rubric, modeling how to use the rubric while also modeling close reading with your graphic novel anchor text. *Note* that you may model filling in the rubric on the board as students watch and participate, and/or you may ask students to fill in their own individual rubrics as you go through this practice so they have a model to refer to if necessary.

Phase 1: Surface Level – What's Happening?

In this first phase, assess what your students were able to garner from the text. In *Soupy Leaves Home*, for example, we see that Pearl is walking out of her home, feeling sad. She can't find warmth, no matter how hard she tries. We see that she hops on a train, gets off somewhere, and steals some clothes. In close-ups, we see her black eye, her anger, pain, and determination. We also see she has a knife and uses it to cut her hair. She looks like a boy now, and we're told this is the story of how she became warm again.

To help your students in this phase, you may ask the following questions:

- What's taking place, where and when is it taking place?
- What Is Pearl doing?
- What is Pearl thinking?
- What is Pearl saying?
- What is Pearl feeling?
- What is the main idea?
- What is the evidence supporting the main idea?
- What are the key details?
- Why are the these details important?

Phase 2: Structure – How Does It Show It? How Does It Say It?

In this phase, students analyze how text, image, and design are used to tell the story. Make sure your students consider how the vocabulary, the font, the page and panel design, and the angles and perspectives presented all help to show and tell what is going on. In the *Soupy Leaves Home* example, we read that Pearl is sadly leaving home because she's tried to make things better but can't. We know Pearl is sad from the text and because she is bent over. On the second page of this example, we see the pain, anger, and determination in her facial expressions and in her body language as she juts her head up forcefully as the train approaches. We see her on the train, leaving home. In a later panel, we see anger and resolve as she takes out her knife to cut her hair. We read that this is the story of how she finds "warmth" again.

(continued)

When discussing this phase, you may want to ask students these questions:

- How do the words tell the story?
- What emotions, thoughts, and actions do the words tell us? What do they imply?
- How does the design (the color, shading, font, and layout) tell the story?
- What emotions, thoughts, and actions do the images and design choices tell us? What do they imply?
- How do the angles in the images change to help us understand what is going on?

Phase 3: Deeper Meaning/Message/Author Intent – What Is the Author Trying to Tell Us?

In this phase, readers analyze the image, text, and design *choices made by the author,* and why the panel or page looks the way it does, in order to find its deep meaning. In the *Soupy Leaves Home* example, the authors have chosen to begin the story in black and olive-green colors. The first page of the story (p. 7) is one large image introducing Pearl leaving home, with text curtly explaining why. Page 9, however, consists of many small panels, including close-ups of Pearl's face and of her clutching a pocketknife, and varied wide-angle shots of her actions. Each panel, perspective, and shot is specific. Each tells us visually and/or verbally what's happening. Each is setting up the plot and showing us who Pearl is. From all this, we infer that she's jumping the train (as she stands between cars), and that she steals clothes from a clothesline (in one shot they're drying on the line and in a later shot she's left her skirt on the ground and, now with short cropped hair, is almost completely dressed in boys' clothing). We infer her mood from the images as well, mainly from her body language and facial expressions.

To help students gain this greater understanding, you may ask the following questions to help them put the author's cues together:

- Why does the text or page look like this (with its particular size or shape)? What do these details tell us and how?
- Why is the image a close-up or wide-angle shot?
- What is the author telling us through the choices she or he made?
- What kinds of inferences (about the story or character) do these choices help us make?
- Why are these details important?

Phase 4: Inspiration – What Can We Learn from This?

This phase gets to the value of the text. This is where we think about the content by asking questions like these:

- What can we learn from this about ourselves and our world?

- How does this change how we think or do things?
- How has the author inspired us? (Basically, this gets to the author's point[s] and what it [they] may mean for us.)

Independent Practice

Introduce the pages 32 and 33 of *Soupy Leaves Home*. Tell the students that after their close reading of pages 7 and 9 together, they are now going to closely read pages 32 and 33 on their own, given the following background:

This story takes place in the 1930s. At that time, many people were homeless. They traveled from place to place looking for food, work, and shelter. They were frequently referred to as *hoboes* and followed their own Hobo Code. In the 1930s, girls were not independent. For Pearl, leaving home as a girl would have been dangerous – hence her transformation. Later, realizing she needs a new name as well as a new appearance, Pearl decides to call herself Soupy.

Looking like a boy, Soupy continues walking along the train tracks. She soon meets an older hobo, who calls himself Ramshackle, and he takes Soupy under his wing. They decide to head south. As they travel, Ramshackle teaches Soupy how to survive.

On pages 32 and 33, we see that as Soupy and Ramshackle continue walking, Ramshackle begins one of many lessons he will teach his companion. Here, the lesson is on self-defense.

Your job now is to use the rubric while analyzing what's happening on pages 32 and 33. Look for clues from the text, images, colors, angles, and panel and page designs. Be your own detectives as you fill in what you understand at the surface level, then at the structure, deeper meaning, and inspiration levels – just as we did together for pages 7 and 9.

Once students have completed the independent practice, meet as a class, and review what they've found.

Lesson Debrief and Assessment

Debrief. Review students' work, discussing the comments and insights they made when filling out their rubrics. You may then want to discuss what cues they used to figure out the different levels of understanding.

Optional. Discuss how these same visual, contextual, and gestural cues might be used by the students when they come across a more challenging text or even in social interactions. What other cues might readers use for greater comprehension? Close the lesson, however, with making sure that students recognize the power of close reading and the steps necessary for close reading.

Assessment. Evaluate students' rubrics and class comments made during the debrief.

Graphic Novels and Literary Devices

Graphic novels offer readers a whole new literary device experience. Their creative combinations of text and images make literary devices more obvious, more concrete, and lots of fun to unearth. From the visual and verbal uses of hyperbole, metaphor, and simile to rolling alliteration and ominous foreshadowing, graphic novels are literary device wonderlands. Let's take a closer look.

Alliteration

While alliteration in graphic novels is predominantly relayed in text, the graphic novel format helps instances of alliteration to stand out. In graphic novels, as the amount of text used is limited to text balloons, alliteration becomes more obvious and recognizable. Figure 6.8 is just one example of how the graphic novel format can highlight alliteration.

FIGURE 6.8 Alliteration in *Hilo: The Boy Who Crashed to Earth*
Source: Judd Winick, *Hilo: The Boy Who Crashed to Earth* (New York: 2015), p. 22, panels 4 and 5.

Hyperbole

Hyperbole is used liberally in graphic novels. Instances can be found in images as well as in text. Here are a few examples:

- In *I Kill Giants* by Joe Kelly and J. M. Ken Nimura, Barbara, a fifth grader, kills giants. In Figure 6.9, we see her battle against a titan as it takes on mythic and epic proportions.

- In *Babymouse: Rock Star*, by Jennifer Holm and Matthew Holm, there is a newspaper article in *Mouse News* headlined "Penny Poodle Dies of Embarrassment!" (p. 20).

- In *The Tweenage Guide to Not Being Unpopular*, by Jimmy Gownley, Amelia asks the reader to imagine the consequences of doing something horrible. Pages 28 to 29 then show all sorts of imaginative and creative hyperbolic images of life's consequences.

- In *Lumberjanes: Beware the Kitten Holy*, by Noelle Stevenson and her coauthors, the counselor, after rescuing her girls in the forest, declares, "That's it. We're going back to the cabin RIGHT NOW. And then I'm locking you all in your cabin and you're NEVER LEAVING AGAIN" (p. 83).

FIGURE 6.9 Hyperbole in *I Kill Giants*
Source: Joe Kelly and J. M. Ken Nimura, *I Kill Giants* (Portland, OR: Image Comics, 2008), p. 123.

Metaphor

Metaphor is an abstract concept that is often difficult for students to grasp. The pairing of image and text in graphic novels makes metaphors more obvious, more concrete, and easier to grasp and remember. Here are a few brilliant examples of the visual and verbal metaphors you'll find in graphic novels:

- *Babymouse: Dragonslayer* by Jennifer Holm and Matthew Holm is all about metaphor. As seen in Figure 6.10, our not-so-fearless protagonist, Babymouse, sets out to slay the (math) dragon and thus "slay" her fear of math. Notice how the operation symbols are arranged as a shield in the middle of page 69 as Babymouse assembles her armor and weapon.

FIGURE 6.10 **Metaphor in *Babymouse: Dragonslayer***
Source: Jennifer Holm and Matthew Holm, *Babymouse: Dragonslayer* (New York: Random House, 2009), pp. 68–69.

- In *El Deafo*, Cece Bell uses metaphor and imagery brilliantly. For example, the character Cece tells us that "being different feels a lot like being alone," while stepping into a "Bubble of Loneliness" (p. 46). Then, in panels 2 and 3 of page 47, she says, "Wherever I am . . ." / ". . . it feels like I'm always inside my bubble."

- Joe Kelly and J. M. Ken Nimura's *I Kill Giants* is all about metaphor. Readers must evaluate whether Barbara is escaping into a world of fantasy, whether this is in fact a story where she kills giants, or whether her quest to kill giants is a metaphor for her difficult life.

- Gene Yang's *American Born Chinese* is another great example. As we see in Figure 6.11, Jin Wang (our protagonist) tells an herbalist that when he grows up, he wants "to be a transformer," which seems innocuous enough because we've seen him just a few pages earlier playing with a transformer toy as he and his parents are driving in a car (moving

FIGURE 6.11 **Metaphor in American Born Chinese**
Source: Gene Luen Yang, *American Born Chinese* (New York: First Second, 2006), p. 27, panels 3 and 4, and p. 194.

to a new home). But we later see the meaning is much deeper as he transforms his outer appearance to look like all the other kids (who are not Chinese).

- In *The United States Constitution: A Graphic Adaptation*, by Jonathan Hennessey and Aaron McConnell, metaphor, art, and prose are used to vividly and concretely explain abstract concepts such as the three-fifths compromise, checks and balances between the three branches of our government, the Electoral College, and why Congress and the American Colonies were a ticking time bomb until necessary compromises were made and the US Constitution was ratified (depicted in Figure 6.12).

FIGURE 6.12 Metaphor, art, and prose illustrate history in *The United States Constitution: A Graphic Adaptation*
Source: Jonathan Hennessey and Aaron McConnell, *The United States Constitution: A Graphic Adaptation* (New York: Hill and Wang, 2008), p. 30.

Foreshadowing

In graphic novels, foreshadowing can be presented through text; through use of design elements such as color, lines, panel frames, and text balloons; and also through specific image content. Such text, design, and illustration choices are used to relay tension and hint at what is to come. Their combined effect allows students to make multiple connections that highlight and reinforce the literary device and content in general.

Figure 6.13, taken from Raina Telgemeier's *Ghosts*, illustrates how text and image can be used to foreshadow what is to come.

In the first panel we read Catrina's comment that "Mom and Dad are dragging us to **this** gloomy place, Bahía de la Luna, California." The image paired with this text shows cars on a

FIGURE 6.13 Foreshadowing in *Ghosts*
Source: Raina Telgemeier, *Ghosts* (New York: Scholastic, 2016), p. 6.

highway, hugging the side of a mountain. We see gray exhaust coming from the cars, and clouds crawling and moving in slowly in the background along the distant valley. We also see shadows from the sun and clouds above the highway and valley. The cars along the highway are driving in this shadow. At this point, the reader is uncertain what exactly to expect, but we are definitely not expecting this to be a sunny, cheery place. While the clouds in the valley seem almost mystical, the suggested shadows from clouds above and unseen seem more foreboding. Even the name, Bahía de la Luna, which translates to Bay of the Moon, carries some mystical or magical connotation.

Also note in Figure 6.13 that the first panel is panoramic and seems to set the scene, depicting where Catrina and her family are heading. The following panels relay action – filling in moment-to-moment actions rather than setting the scene. We can also note that the page's remaining panels support the impression set in the first panel.

LESSON: FUN WITH LITERARY DEVICES (JIGSAW ACTIVITY)

Mastery Objective. Students will gain experience recognizing, understanding, and differentiating literary devices, and will more fully understand how these devices influence the storytelling and reading experience.

Materials Needed

- Anchor text(s) with examples of the literary device(s) you plan to discuss (feel free to use one of the texts suggested earlier or to find your own).

- Access to a variety of graphic novels your students can search through to explore various authors' uses of literary devices.

Introducing the Lesson

Review, define, and/or explain what literary devices are, and how they influence comprehension, memory, and storytelling.

Guided Practice (a whole class activity)

Use your anchor text(s) to demonstrate how literary devices are used by the author(s). Discuss how these literary devices help shape the story and the reading experience.

Independent Practice

Divide students into a few groups. Assign each group a graphic novel (one that you've vetted and that has examples of the literary device that group is targeting), *or* let students explore a variety of graphic novels you or your school librarian have selected. Have students rifle through the graphic novels on a "literary treasure hunt," searching for as many

(continued)

examples of their assigned literary device as they can find. Then meet together as a class, with each group presenting the examples they found.

Alternate Suggested Lesson

With your students, create a story line in which there are dire consequences. Then divide the class into groups, with each group focusing on a specific literary device (for example, foreshadowing, hyperbole, alliteration, simile, and/or metaphor). Direct each group of students to brainstorm examples of how they might use their specific literary device when telling this story in a graphic novel panel (or panels). Then come together, having each group share their work. Discuss which literary devices seemed to work best or least, and why.

Lesson Debrief and Assessment

With your students' examples written on the board or displayed with an overhead projector, discuss them. You may want to discuss these issues:

- The images and emotions these examples suggest.

- How these examples change the reading experience.

- What examples of literary devices the students like, and what ones they don't like, and why.

- How your students might edit or improve upon the examples they don't like.

Evaluate the quality and quantity of the literary devices found by each group, as well as each group's contributions and comments in the class discussion.

Graphic Novels and Character Development

A final benefit of teaching reading with graphic novels is that they make it easier for students to observe and chart character development. Graphic novels' visual element and the fact that readers must literally construct their understanding of both story and character also make it easier to understand and identify with diverse characters.

While graphic novels tend to have all sorts of vibrant characters, the following books (also described in the Bonus Resource) are some of our favorite character-driven stories. Their characters are multifaceted, and we discover some exciting twists and surprises as we get to know them: *Babymouse* (grades 2–6); *Hilo* (grades 2–5); *Monster on the Hill* (grades 3+); *El Deafo* (grades 3–6); the *Amelia Rules!* series (grades 4+); *Real Friends* (grades 3–6); *All's Faire in Middle School* (grades 3–8); *American Born Chinese* (grades 5+); *Boxers and Saints* (grades 5+); *Nimona* (grades 4+); *The P.L.A.I.N. Janes* (grades 7+); *Rust* (grades 4+); and *Nothing Can Possibly Go Wrong* (grades 6+).

LESSON: GOOD VERSUS EVIL

In the following lesson, we examine "good" versus "evil" characters as we take a closer look at these qualities in specific graphic novel characters. For this lesson, you may choose any graphic novel with strong characters, although we've suggested *Monster on the Hill* for younger students (grades 2–4) and *Nimona* for older students (grades 4+).

We've chosen *Monster on the Hill*, by Rob Harrell (Top Shelf Books), because if offers a wonderful twist on evil dragons: in this story, their fire-breathing and destructive rampages have intrinsic value. The problem for one town, however, is that its dragon just isn't evil enough. To help him find his inner evil, the town sends its discredited doctor to "cure" this dragon. Note that *Monster on the Hill*, while recommended for younger readers, is such a strong story it can be used for all ages.

That said, for older and more sophisticated readers, we also recommend *Nimona*. *Nimona* is about a confident, snarky, inspiring shape-shifter named Nimona, who ostensibly serves as sidekick to super-villain Lord Ballister. Lord Ballister is a disfigured knight who had to leave the Institution of Law Enforcement and Heroics after losing his arm in a joust against Sir Ambrosius Goldenloin. Subsequently, he becomes an evil scientist whose only goal is to defame Sir Ambrosius Goldenloin and to expose and destroy the Institution of Law Enforcement and Heroics. Readers, however, soon find out that no one is who they seem to be. Even good versus evil becomes distorted. Even more fascinating – and engaging – is that the more we read about Nimona and see her in action, the less we know or understand who or what exactly she is. All we know is that we're constantly rooting for her and can't quite get enough.

Mastery Objective. To take a close look at a book's characters: how they grow (or don't grow) when facing challenges, and how we as readers come to the story with our own expectations and labels (such as "good" and "evil") that can often be deceptive and manipulated.

Materials Needed

- A selected graphic novel with strong characters and character twists (for example, *Monster on the Hill* or *Nimona*).

- The Character Development Analysis Worksheet. Hand out one copy of the worksheet for each character you wish your students to analyze.

Introducing the Lesson

Come up with a class definition of what constitutes a "good" character and what constitutes an "evil" character, and how we often label them as heroes or villains, respectively. You may also want students to share examples of their favorite "good" and "bad" guys. Discuss these issues:

- The roles good and evil characters and heroes and villains play in students' favorite stories.

(continued)

- Do we like or dislike heroes? Why? Do we like or dislike villains? Why?

- How do these characters help tell a story or relay a point or lesson?

- How can we tell a "good" from an "evil" character? Should we label them like this?

Guided Practice

Have students read the selected graphic novel. You may want to assign roles and have students read their selected parts out loud (character parts, narrator parts, sound effect parts, etc.) and together as a class. Another option is to have them read the graphic novel silently or previously for homework. A third option is to do a little of both – reading most of it independently and then coming together and reading it aloud as a class.

Once your students have read the book, you may want to revisit your earlier questions about good versus evil roles and characters with reference to this particular story.

Once you've revisited good versus evil, begin to fill in the Character Development Analysis Worksheet. You may want to fill in a worksheet for each good or evil character, or you may simply select one character to observe and analyze. We recommend that you discuss each of the "story/character elements" in the first column, and then begin to fill in related textual and visual elements found in the beginning of the story for a few of the story/character elements.

Note: This Character Development Analysis Worksheet can be found in a reproducible format on our websites (www.wiley.com/go/worthathousandwords, meryljaffe.com, and taliahurwich.com)

Notes on filling in the Character Development Analysis Worksheet:

- Note that the table is divided into three major sections.

- The first section, the column on the left, lists different types of story/character elements. There is space in each of the boxes for students to fill them in appropriately. For example, "physical elements" are the character's physical qualities (eyes, hair, body build, etc.); "likes" and "dislikes" are the things the character likes and doesn't like; "motivation" is what it is that drives the character to do what he or she does so well (or not so well); and so forth.

- The second section, in the middle of the worksheet, asks students to find supporting *textual* evidence that relays each of the story/character elements listed to the left. Have students record textual evidence (when available) for each element they list.

- The third section, on the right-hand side, asks students to find *visual* evidence that relays each of the story/character elements listed to the far left. Have students record visual evidence (when available) for each element they list.

- The second and third sections have three columns each. These columns ask for textual or visual evidence from the beginning of the story, the middle of the story, and the end of the story – allowing students to observe how, where, and when the characters change.

Character Development Analysis Worksheet

Student Name _____

Character Name _____

Book _____

Story/character element	Supporting evidence found in the *text*			Supporting evidence found in the *images*		
	Beginning	Middle	End	Beginning	Middle	End
Physical elements:						
Likes:						
Dislikes:						
External conflict:						
Internal conflict:						
Strengths:						
Weaknesses:						
Motivation:						
Figurative language used:						

Independent Practice

Have students continue to chart and analyze the characters' development. You may want to divide your students into two groups. One group that analyzes the "good" character while the other analyzes the "bad" character. Or you may want them all to analyze both characters.

(continued)

Lesson Debrief and Assessment

Debrief. If you assigned students to different characters, have each group present their findings, discussing each of the distinctive character elements and how they changed over the course of the story. If you had students analyze all the designated characters, review each one, discussing their distinctive character elements and how they changed. Discuss how the author used or manipulated readers' perceptions of these characters.

Once you've analyzed what makes these characters tick and how they changed, revisit your earlier, introductory discussion questions. Have your responses changed a bit? Why? Why not? You may also want to discuss how graphic novels use both visual and textual elements to tell the story and develop the characters. Does the dual presentation of text and image help us to gain a deeper understanding of the characters? Why or why not?

Assessment. Evaluate the depth and details provided in students' Character Development Analysis Worksheets as well as their contributions and comments in the class discussion.

As we close this chapter, we hope we have helped you obtain a better feel for how to select and use graphic novels for your reading and reading comprehension classes. Please refer to the Bonus Resource for help with selecting the graphic novels for your particular lessons and diverse student body, and please take some time to explore the resources mentioned in Appendix B. They have some wonderful links with additional lesson and text suggestions.

GRAPHIC NOVELS AND THE WRITING PROCESS

Writing is probably one of the most demanding skills we ask of our students. It requires creativity, critical thinking, memory, attention to sequences and details, a substantial lexicon of words (and spelling), and knowing *what* to say and *how* best to say it. Graphic novels present unique and innovative opportunities for students to develop elements of their writing. In some cases, these texts make abstractions more concrete as they separate storytelling components into more obvious and observable units. In other cases, they make storytelling elements (setting, for example) more focused and engaging. This chapter focuses on how you might use graphic novels to develop, enhance, and/or refine your students' writing and prewriting skills and make students more comfortable with writing decisions and the writing process in general. We present several suggestions on how to use graphic novels for brainstorming, pacing, character development, and general writing skills that can be used – whether one is writing prose fiction, graphic novels or comics, expository materials, and/or persuasive nonfiction.

Before we begin, however, we raise one more issue about teaching writing. To fit everything needful into writing curricula, teachers often ask students to make decisions quickly during the writing process. As a result, you'll find certain students agonizing over the decisions they have to make, leaving them less time to work on their actual writing. One way to get students acclimated to making quick writing decisions (without agonizing over them) during the writing process is to give students a lot of quick writing prompts that allow them to experiment, make mistakes, more comfortably take risks, and be able to use their better work in later, larger projects or be able to shrug off work they are not satisfied with as a less-than-successful experiment. Many teachers call these activities "warm-up activities." Talia likes to use the term *brain dumps*, to make them feel even more informal. It further emphasizes that this is a chance for students to write whatever pops into their brains. In accord with this view, we will provide you with many writing prompts you can use in your curriculum to give students an opportunity to quickly practice different skills useful for the writing process. These aren't formal lesson activities, so they should not be used for formal instruction or assessment – simply as a means of letting students practice writing skills in a low-key environment. We hope that you'll intersperse them with larger writing lessons on a fairly regular basis.

Here are some guidelines for using quick writing prompts as brain dumps:

- Each brain dump activity should take around 15 minutes. The more regular these activities are, the more students will become accustomed to filling those 15 minutes.

- While these activities should *not* be formally evaluated, feel free to let students know what worked well.

- If a brain dump includes a drawing element, add about 5 minutes and explicitly tell the students that they only have time for simple drawings or sketches.

- Students will most likely not finish what they've been working on, and that is perfectly fine. If there were any particular writing prompts they enjoyed, let the students know that they can finish and edit their written piece at a later time.

- Ideally, provide a few minutes after the students have written their brain dumps to share at least one student's work with the class. Alternatively, set aside around 15 minutes at the end of the week for everyone to share a brain dump of her or his choice.

Using Graphic Novels to Teach Writing Prose Fiction

There are many skills students need to master to write sophisticated works of fiction. For example, students must create three-dimensional characters and then decide how best to relay their characters' conflicts, strengths, affinities, and flaws as these figures navigate through a hopefully gripping plot. They must establish realistic settings and must set a pace that moves their work along, while slowing down when necessary to highlight critical junctures or emotions. Further, details must be accurate, clear, and convincing while engaging and relatable. A work of prose fiction will have a unique setting, cast of characters, and plot, yet many different readers will have to relate to these people, their desires, and their dilemmas.

In this section, we will explore how graphic novels can help you teach some of the skills needed to create compelling fiction. The skills that we focus on are often overlooked in syllabi, and we will talk about why these unique skills are important for the larger writing process, how graphic novels can be used to teach and reinforce them, and some potential writing prompts you can use as brain dumps to help your students practice these skills.

Envisioning Characters

One can learn a lot about a character based on how he or she looks and, perhaps more importantly, how the character chooses to look. For example, consider the appearance of Barbara, the protagonist in the graphic novel *I Kill Giants*, in Figure 7.1.

This outfit is her everyday outfit, and immediately we can learn a lot about her. We see in this image that Barbara is a bit eccentric (rabbit ears, heart-shaped pocket book, bowling shirt

FIGURE 7.1 Barbara's Everyday Appearance in *I Kill Giants*
Source: Joe Kelly and J. M. Ken Nimura, *I Kill Giants* (Berkeley, CA: Image Comics, 2009), p. 7.

combination) and independent – she isn't concerned with her peers' sense of fashion. Then there is the way she chooses to stand – with one foot out, hands on her hips, and a slight frown on her face. Her clothes, her posture, her expression, her choices, all show she is determined, different, and proud. This may mean that she's not popular, that she may be standoffish, and that she may sometimes be alone. We also see that with the exception of her heart-shaped pocketbook, she wears clothes that are tomboyish. She may be more comfortable hanging out with boys than girls. However, she's not dressed like she's up for playing sports: the bunny ears would get in the way and her hair is not tied behind her. We get a sense that she's a bit nerdy from this and also from the large glasses. In short, you get a sense of who Barbara is as a character just by looking at her.

Often when students write prose fiction, they give little thought to what their characters look like, save for their height, eyes, and hair. To some degree, spending a whole paragraph on what a character wears each day might seem a waste of time. But in the prewriting process, information such as characters' sense of fashion, their scars, how they wear their hair, how they stand or sit, and other physical characteristics is crucial if readers are to understand and relate to them.

Working with graphic novels can help writers create and envision their characters. They might, for example, want to scan through a few different graphic novels to help develop a sense of who their characters are, what they wear, and so on. Writers might also draw a major or pivotal character doing mundane activities in several panels as a means of brainstorming – because when they don't have to keep the plot in mind, they can focus on *who* that character really is in his or her daily life). To help students create their characters, you may also want to use websites such as pixton.com; ToonDoo.com; MakeBeliefsComix.com; and www.canva.com/create/comic-strips. Of course, the old-fashioned way of simply drawing characters also works.

Here are some writing prompts and brain dumps that you can use to help your students practice envisioning their characters:

- Sketch how your character would dress for her or his birthday party. Write out the character's thought process in deciding how to dress for the party, keeping in mind what she or he might be doing at that birthday party.

- Sketch how your character would look on a normal weekday.

- Assume your character has a scar. Write about where the scar is, and how the character got that scar.

- Think about the things your character never leaves home without. Draw them, and describe one of them in detail.

- Your character just got transferred to a school that requires school uniforms. Write about your character's reaction and how that character makes the uniform his or her own. For example, you can write about the way in which character might try to break the uniform dress code, accessorize the uniform, arrange his or her hair, select shoes to wear, choose a bag and notebook, or do anything else in relation to the uniform.

- It's Halloween. Who or what is your character dressing up as? Why?

Establishing a Setting

We all live and breathe in settings. Everywhere we go, visit, shop, walk, and interact is a setting. With each setting we encounter, we are often expected to behave in certain ways based on who we are and why we're there. As a result, clear settings are crucial when composing a scene. Each setting provides a writer with a set of roles and expectations that are typically placed on anyone in that setting. For instance, if Little Red Riding Hood were to come across a wolf in a lawyer's office (instead of in a forest), she might react differently. When a writer follows the roles and expectations of his or her settings, the narrative becomes more believable and easier to comprehend. When a writer chooses to have his or her characters realistically break from those expectations, it can surprise and potentially engage the reader further. Although if those setting deviations are not written so as to be realistic, they may just as easily frustrate the reader.

Setting becomes even more important when writers are using less commonplace settings. In fantasy, for instance, the setting gives the reader a sense of how similar to or different from our world the protagonist's world is, helping to explain the decisions and conflicts that face him or her. In a mystery, the setting gives us clues (and misdirections) about things that don't fit and, more importantly, that lead to the mystery's resolution. In historical fiction, the setting brings us to a different time, showing us how the world was different and how historical figures both made sense of their world and shaped it into the world we know today.

Graphic novels are great tools to help students better understand how to establish setting. In prose fiction, writing a paragraph – or even a sentence – describing the setting often pauses the action. As a result, descriptions of critical settings may not appear often in your students' work. In graphic novels, however, the setting is ever-present visually. Depending on the writer's intention for any given panel, it will be in either the background or the foreground.

Here are some writing prompts and brain dumps that you can use to help your students practice developing and making full use of setting in their work:

- Sketch your setting at its messiest. Then imagine how a janitor, a street cleaner, a parent, or a kid who has to clean this setting reacts. Write from that person's perspective.

- The Queen of England is visiting your setting. Sketch how the setting changes because of her visit, and write, from her perspective, her impression of the place.

- An alien is visiting your setting, with no knowledge of what this place is and who the people are in it. Write from the alien's perspective what he observes and what he thinks about the events.

- Write a day in the life from the perspective of the setting.

- Sketch a setting. Write about the first time your protagonist is in this setting. What are his or her first impressions?

- Sketch how your setting looks in the morning, at noon, and at night. Show how it looks different at each time of the day. How does it look in different seasons?

- Write any scene in a setting, using second person narration and without explicitly telling readers where they are. So the readers can figure out where they are, you will have to be as descriptive as possible.

Understanding Pacing

No matter the medium or genre one is writing for, pacing is immensely important when telling a story or relaying an incident. We've all had students who would happily spend the first seven pages of their 10-page short story just writing exposition. We've also all had students who would happily write no exposition whatsoever save a single establishing sentence (such as, "One day we went to the beach") before going into the action. It is important to help students think more strategically about how to lay out the telling or retelling of an event or scene, be it fictional or real. Students should be mindful of how long their introductory and concluding paragraphs should be, and how much page space should be devoted to each part of their argument or story. This is a skill that requires a fair amount of higher-order cognition, planning, and executive function and, as a result, is something students often struggle with. However, it is also a skill that can be demonstrated and practiced using graphic novels.

Pacing in graphic novels is much more apparent than in prose. You see pacing through seeing how many panels are devoted to a setting or to a moment of action. Because so much is inferred in the panels and the gutters of a graphic novel, writers need to strategically think not simply about what they need to show but also about how much time they need to spend unfolding the scene and how long they'd like the reader to spend looking at the panel (or panels) depicting it.

Let's take a closer look at pacing by examining two pages from *Snow White: A Graphic Novel*, shown in Figure 7.2. This graphic novel is a retelling of the classic fairy tale, set in Depression-era New York City. It is a fantastic graphic novel and can be used in many ways in any language arts or social studies classroom. One thing of note about this graphic novel is that it's created to mimic film noir, where pacing and atmosphere are extremely important.

On the pages displayed in Figure 7.2, the evil stepmother is consulting with her magic mirror, which in this retelling appears as her magic stock ticker. What is particularly noticeable about the pacing is that so little seems to happen over the course of these two pages. Instead, the pacing has been slowed in order to raise tension by creating small mysteries the reader has to solve.

The pages start with a small panel of the stepmother looking at a strip of paper, and we can't tell what it is. The second panel establishes what she's seeing: the paper tape from a stock ticker, with stock names, symbols, and numbers showing how the stocks are performing. That's one "mystery" solved, but it raises the next question: why is she looking at this? We aren't initially given an answer. Instead, the panel brings us back to the stepmother's perspective: we are reading the ticker tape at the same time and pace that the stepmother is reading it. Except as we continue to read, one mystery is substituted by another mystery: this is no ordinary stock ticker. The symbols are getting smudged for no apparent reason. In the next panel – a close-up of her small beady eyes – we see that she's getting quite angry, creating more confusion and mystery. We get answers only toward the end of the page: the words "most . . . beautiful." Even then, we have to infer from what we know of the original Snow White story and the stepmother's reaction that this is the magic

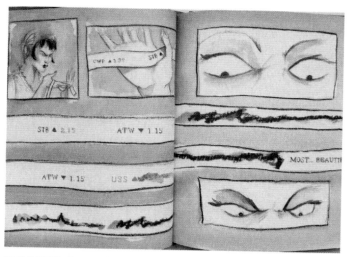

FIGURE 7.2 *Snow White: A Graphic Novel*
Source: Matt Phelan, *Snow White: A Graphic Novel* (Somerville, MA: Candlewick Press, 2016), pp. 42–43.

mirror telling the evil stepmother that she's no longer the most beautiful woman in the land. We are now presented with the main plot and are excited to turn the page.

The reveal is fairly surprising – a direct result of slowing down enough to build several smaller mysteries and creating tension for the reader. Creating tension in this story could be a particularly tricky job: how do you create suspense in a story everyone already knows? By slowing down the pacing, author Matt Phelan creates new tensions that rely on the fact that we're familiar with the story and looking to figure out what is going on.

While in this *Snow White* example the pace slows down, pacing in storytelling can speed up action as well (think of a montage in a film for an example). Every writer needs to understand that part of the writing process is not only writing out what happens, but knowing how much time the reader should spend in that moment and what the consequences of spending that much time would be. The following sample lesson focuses on pacing as a deliberate choice. Its intention is to get students thinking about how and why they would want to make moments in a story longer or shorter.

LESSON: PACING IN *LITTLE RED RIDING HOOD*

In this sample lesson, we're using the same moment in the story *Little Red Riding Hood* that we used in our sample lesson in Chapter 5, on motivation. Feel free to change the scene you will use with your students to a moment in a story that your students have just read. Make sure, however, that it's not a climactic moment in the story.

Mastery Objective. Students will learn how and why to slow down or speed up certain moments in a story.

Materials Needed

Each student will need several sheets of blank, unlined paper.

Introducing the Lesson

Instruct students they are about to participate in an activity where they will have to present a moment in a story in one panel, then three panels, and then five panels. Tell them that creating five panels for one particular moment can be challenging, so the class will first work through an example together. Our suggested example: the start of class.

Guided Practice

Write on the board: "The Start of Class: One Panel."

Ask students what they'd show if they were to depict the start of class in one graphic novel panel. Record their decision.

Then, write "Three Panels" on the board and ask the students how they would extend that moment into a progression of three panels (for example: the bell rings in the first

(continued)

panel, the students sit down in the next one, and they take out their class materials in the final one).

Finally, repeat this process for five panels. Before students work independently, ask them what strategies they used to help them out with this exercise.

Independent Practice

Students individually present a scene from *Little Red Riding Hood* in one, three, and then five panels; we suggest the scene when Little Red Riding Hood first meets the wolf in the forest.

Lesson Debrief and Assessment

Debrief. When students are finished with their panels, have them share their work. Discuss the challenges they faced with this activity, and how they overcame those challenges. Ask students why they might want to present a moment in a story over the course of five panels, and why they might want to present a moment in a story in just one panel. Transition this conversation into a discussion of thinking strategically about what moments are important in a story and when it's prudent to extend those moments and why. Make it a point to talk with students about how they can take this lesson and apply it to prose writing.

Assessment. Have students write an outline or storyboard (if you've taught them to storyboard, a technique discussed later in this chapter) for their next big writing project, where they map out the plot elements as well as how many paragraphs and/or how many pages or paragraphs they plan to use for these moments. Make sure the students are mindful of not only how important each plot point is but also how confusing a particular moment might be for potential readers, and whether they will need extra space to ensure that the moment is less confusing.

The previous sections have discussed how to think about using graphic novels to teach writing fiction. Some of these ideas can be applied to nonfiction writing as well, but writing nonfiction requires a set of skills that are both similar to and different from writing fiction, as we discuss in the next section.

Using Graphic Novels to Teach Writing Prose Nonfiction

Just as there are different types of fiction (fantasy, realistic fiction, historical fiction, and so forth), there are different types of nonfiction. In the following list, we outline the characteristics of four major categories of nonfiction. In the remainder of this nonfiction section, we will focus on two of these four types.

1. *Creative nonfiction* (aka narrative nonfiction). These are nonfiction works written using the same conventions used in fiction. Notable types of creative nonfiction are biography

and memoir. While there are a lot of fantastic graphic novel biographies and memoirs (many of which you'll find in the Bonus Resource), we will not be focusing on how to write creative nonfiction, largely because this can be taught in a way similar to teaching the writing of fiction.

2. *Descriptive nonfiction* (aka illustrative nonfiction). These are nonfiction works that vividly describe something. A notable example is the travelogue. This type of nonfiction writing is rarely done in school settings and, as a result, will not be explicitly discussed. However, we would like to note that the graphic novel format can be aligned very nicely with the requirement to describe something in great detail.

3. *Expository nonfiction* (aka informational nonfiction). These are nonfiction works that share information about something without presenting an argument. Notable examples of expository nonfiction are newspaper articles and, in most cases, book reports.

4. *Persuasive nonfiction* (aka argumentative nonfiction). The name is fairly self-explanatory: these are nonfiction works that present information in order to make an argument or persuade the reader about something. As students become more accomplished essay writers, their essays should not only present facts but also become works of persuasive nonfiction. Notable examples of persuasive nonfiction are the opinion pieces found on newspapers' editorial pages.

We will be focusing here on expository and persuasive nonfiction. More specifically, we will talk about the importance of sequencing and contextualizing when writing these types of nonfiction, and how graphic novels can be used to help students grasp these concepts when writing nonfiction.

Sequencing

How writers sequence the content of their writing is critical for fiction and nonfiction writing. When writing nonfiction, however, there's the additional challenge of needing to sequence facts. With a story or with creative writing, readers are used to filling in gaps and strategically placed jumps in time. With nonfiction, however, the proper sequencing and presentation of facts or timelines is crucial to relaying events, arguments, and/or actions readers may not yet know about.

Structure and sequencing are particularly critical when writing persuasive nonfiction. This is probably why the three and five paragraph essays we teach are so helpful. They come with a definitive structure and organization to follow. The student begins with an introductory paragraph and thesis statement, continues with the body of the essay, and ends with a concluding paragraph summing up critical points or arguments. Straying from that sequence, while not necessarily affecting the logic of an argument, may confuse the reader and minimalize the content's desired impact. Furthermore, each paragraph has its own sequence, starting with a topic sentence and ending with a concluding sentence that transitions to the next paragraph.

Graphic novels are great tools to teach sequencing. Cutting up existing graphic novel pages, for example, and having students observe and manipulate various panel sequence options can help them better understand how critical this skill is. The sequence of panels is deliberate, and any other sequence obfuscates the narrative. The following sample lesson is meant to make the importance of sequencing more explicit for your students.

Lesson: Sequencing

Mastery Objective. Students will recognize the importance of sequencing to relaying important information.

Materials Needed

- For guided practice option 1, a copy of the "In case of fire . . ." image (Figure 7.3).

Note: Figure 7.3 "In case of fire" can be found in a reproducible format on our websites (www.wiley.com/go/worthathousandwords, meryljaffe.com, and taliahurwich.com)

FIGURE 7.3   In case of fire . . .
Source: Photo courtesy of Scott McCloud.

- For guided practice option 2, four emoji printed out large enough for the whole class to see from their seats, and Scotch tape or some other means of arranging the emoji on the board so that you can change their order throughout the lesson. See the accompanying emoji examples.

Note: These four emoji can be found in a reproducible format on our websites (www .wiley.com/go/worthathousandwords, meryljaffe.com, and taliahurwich.com)

- Emoji #1:   - Emoji #3:

- Emoji #2:   - Emoji #4:

- For independent practice, unlined paper, and envelopes with several panels cut out of a graphic novel; you will need one envelope for each group of four students.

Introducing the Lesson

Discuss with your students how the order in which a writer presents information influences the way that a reader understands and appreciates that content.

Guided Practice Option 1 (for older students)

Display Figure 7.3, the "In case of fire . . ." image.

Ask students what they think the image is saying, and how they came up with that interpretation. Ask if there is any other way the sign might be interpreted, and why. Make sure to point out that the image by itself (designed to aid non-English speakers), despite including the recognizable icons for fire safety instructions (a person, fire, and something that goes up and down), is extremely confusing. The box with up and down arrows might be an elevator, but the two parallel diagonal lines make the image less iconic and more confusing. The person is using the stairs (not the elevator), but might be seen as using the stairs to get to the elevator, in which there are already three other people. Furthermore, he might be seen as running from a smaller fire toward a larger fire.

Ask students what messages an individual might receive from such an image. For example, Scott McCloud posed such a question on his Twitter account, and one (humorous) response was "Use chopsticks to remove cooked children from hot oven."

Next, draw each of the image elements from this sign on the board. Experiment with how to arrange them so they make more sense. Finally, have the class come up with their own best solution, one that even an alien would understand.

Guided Practice Option 2 (for younger students)

Share the four emoji with students.

Ask the students what story is being told with these emoji (one reading is that two people graduate and there's a party – perhaps in honor of the graduation – and then everyone goes to sleep).

Ask students what would happen if they left one of the four emoji out. Ask students what stories may be told with only the three remaining emoji. For example, what happens when the graduation emoji is omitted? List on the board as many possible stories as the students can think of. Depending on your students, you may want to specify what would happen if you were to leave out the graduation emoji, as an example.

Then, ask what would happen if they changed the order of the emoji. For example, what story is told when the sleep emoji is placed before the party emoji instead of after? What happens when the happy emoji is placed as the last emoji instead of the second?

Independent Practice

Tell students that in groups of four, they will get an envelope with panels from a graphic novel that you've copied and cut out. Instruct them to guess the correct order of the

(continued)

panels and be able to discuss how the story they came up with would change or become less clear in the following situations:

- The order of the panels is changed.

- One of the panels is omitted.

Have students present their findings to the class when they're finished.

Lesson Debrief and Assessment

Debrief. Discuss with students how sequencing effects nonfiction writing. What are some lessons from this that can be applied to writing nonfiction?

Assessment. Have students open a draft of the current nonfiction piece they've been writing, and have them create a reverse outline of that piece. In a reverse outline, they should summarize every paragraph they wrote as a single sentence and then order these sentences like an outline. (If you haven't covered outlines with your students, they could present these sentences as a flowchart or as visual thumbnails* in order to present the flow of ideas). At home, have students prepare written comments reflecting on their reverse outlines. For example, what about their sequence worked well? Should anything be moved earlier or later in their written work? Does anything need to be added? Is anything unnecessary and could be omitted?

If you decide to use this lesson to introduce nonfiction writing, then at this point introduce a nonfiction topic for students to write about. Have them present what they plan to write as an outline, a flowchart, or visual thumbnails in order to display the flow of their ideas.

Evaluate their assessment assignments for clarity of sequence as well as clarity of content.

*Thumbnails are small, simple images or doodles used by storyboard artists, graphic designers, and writers to represent the different parts of their work and then organize that work. This allows them to explore multiple sequencing ideas quickly, as the thumbnails can be easily seen and rearranged.

Giving Enough Background Information

Regardless of what type of nonfiction a student is writing, providing background information is critical. In expository writing, for example, notice how much of a newspaper story is devoted to explanatory details. A writer not only needs to provide background information to support the *who*, *what*, *where*, *when*, and *why* of the story; she or he also needs to include the *how*, as well as provide necessary information about the quotes used. Even in persuasive nonfiction, where the purpose is to persuade and not teach, background information is necessary for several reasons. First, such data can be used to demonstrate why a reader should care about the writer's argument. Second, data can be used to make each argument the writer ultimately wants to use understandable and convincing.

The challenge for writers is recognizing what background information is necessary, particularly if they're novice writers or if they're not familiar with the audience's basic understanding of their topic. We demonstrate the importance of supplying background information and knowing your audience in the following mini-lesson. Feel free to tweak it or to use it as is.

LESSON: THE IMPORTANCE OF BACKGROUND INFORMATION AND KNOWING YOUR AUDIENCE

Mastery Objective. Students will learn to think critically about background information, why it's important, and why it's important to know one's audience.

Note: Figures 7.4 and 7.5 can be found in a reproducible format on our websites (www.wiley.com/go/worthathousandwords, meryljaffe.com, and taliahurwich.com)

Materials Needed

▪ Handout images from Nathan Hale's *Treaties, Trenches, Mud, and Blood* (p. 6), shown in Figures 7.4 and 7.5.

▪ Two highlighters of different colors for each student.

FIGURE 7.4   *Treaties, Trenches, Mud, and Blood* (top of p. 6)
Source: Nathan Hale, *Treaties, Trenches, Mud, and Blood* (A World War I Tale),
Nathan Hale's Hazardous Tales #4 (New York: Abrams, 2014), p. 6.

Introducing the Lesson

▪ Tell students that you're going to read and talk about a selection from one of Nathan Hale's Hazardous Tales. Feel free to give as much background information about the

(continued)

FIGURE 7.5   *Treaties, Trenches, Mud, and Blood* (bottom of p. 6).
Source: Nathan Hale, *Treaties, Trenches, Mud, and Blood* (A World War I Tale),
Nathan Hale's Hazardous Tales #4 (New York: Abrams, 2014), p. 6.

graphic novel's characters and overall story line (as presented in the next bullet point) as you'd like.

Background. Nathan Hale's Hazardous Tales is a series that depicts events from American history with fun facts, humor, and wordplay. The series begins as Nathan Hale, the first American spy, is about to be hung by the British (by a hangman and with a British provost there to witness the act). As the Hangman prepares to fulfill his role, Hale is struck by a giant magical book of America's history – as a sort of gift for the life he's about to give for his country. When asked if he has any last words, Hale starts telling the Hangman (who becomes a wonderful foil in the series) and the Provost stories he has garnered from the book of what is to come.

Guided Practice

Hand out the copies of Figure 7.4. Read the panels out loud as a class, with one student reading for the Hangman, one student reading for the British officer (also referred to as Provost), and you reading for Nathan Hale. Tell the students that you're reading for Hale because there are a lot of difficult words and phrases to read and you want to make sure they're relayed correctly.

After reading through Figure 7.4, tell the students that Hale is deliberately making this section confusing to his readers by including words and phrases that only certain experts would understand. That is, he *wants* students to be confused.

Have students quickly and silently highlight the words and phrases that Nathan Hale says in the second row of panels that they don't understand. Remind them that they cannot highlight whole sentences. If they are struggling with a particular sentence, they need to figure out what words in the sentence make the sentence confusing. When the students are finished, quickly get a few examples of words or phrases they highlighted.

Hand out Figure 7.5, telling students that these panels come right after the panels in Figure 7.4. Instruct students to highlight in a different color everything the Provost didn't understand. Share student answers regarding what the Provost didn't understand, comparing this to what the Hangman didn't understand. Have students reflect on this. Why do they think the Provost was so much more knowledgeable than the Hangman?

Be sure to tell the students at some point during the conversation that simply giving enough clear and understandable information to explain what Nathan Hale says on this page takes about 25 pages in the graphic novel.

Discuss with students what lessons they learned from this activity that they can apply to their own writing. What mistakes does the character Nathan Hale make as he begins telling the story of World War I? How can they avoid making those mistakes when they're writing?

Independent Practice

Assign a persuasive nonfiction writing assignment. Allow students to complete it in prose or in graphic novel format. Before writing, however, they must outline

- their main position;

- their target audience;

- what they expect their target audience to already know; and

- what facts they will have to teach their target audience in order to make their argument.

Debrief and Assessment

Have students share their outlines with the class, making sure they explain why they chose the target audience they chose and why they are including the specific facts and points they include. Discuss and evaluate their choices. Do they expect to be writing to someone like the Hangman or like the Provost? Evaluate the assignment on how closely they met the assignment demands and how appropriate their choices were.

Using Images and Imagery to Provide Information

Mitochondria are the powerhouses of the cell.

News media is the fourth branch of government.

Learning is a journey.

When we present information, we often find metaphors to help explain complex concepts and emphasize particularly important points to get across. When we use metaphors, we do so because they make certain facts easier to communicate. Graphic novels are great examples of texts that communicate metaphors in nonfiction (and fiction) writing. In nonfiction, however, metaphors are particularly helpful as they make what may be dry or complicated material much more accessible, understandable, and often more memorable. Consider, for example, the panel from Jonathan Hennessey and Aaron McConnell's *The United States Constitution: A Graphic Adaptation*, shown in Figure 7.6.

FIGURE 7.6 *The United States Constitution: A Graphic Adaptation*
Source: Jonathan Hennessey and Aaron McConnell, *The United States Constitution:
A Graphic Adaptation* (New York: Hill and Wang: 2008), p. 34.

By comparing Congressmen and Congresswomen to relay racers and comparing Senators to long-distance runners, Hennessey makes his concluding sentence – "the Senate [is] more stable and less reactive to changes in the mood of the country" – more understandable and approachable for a wide variety of readers. Students, particularly those under the age of 18 who have never had to vote, may not have given much thought to American politics. However, all have run relay races as well as regular races.

For example, in a relay race, as in the House of Representatives, the success of the person running before a specific racer makes a big difference. That is, if the racer is on a team that's farther ahead than other teams, there's no pressure to catch up, leading perhaps to a pace that is more conservative than a flat-out sprint. Similarly, if a political party feels that it's doing well, it may feel less pressure to be as reactive to trends and growing its political power, vying instead to simply maintain what it currently has. In this way and others, members of the House of Representatives can be more reactive to current circumstances. Further, since each leg of a relay race often covers a shorter distance than a non-relay race, relay racers are more ready to sprint and exert as much energy as they can. This is similar to the House of Representatives being less stable than the Senate – House members are trying to enact laws over a much shorter time. They may also prefer working on bills with short-term gains (which will be seen by the next election) as opposed to those with longer and more sustainable gains.

Continuing the metaphor, comparing Senate races to a long-distance race allows the reader to respect why the Senate is more stable. In a longer race, a runner appropriately paces him- or herself. If long-distance racers expend all their energy in the first tenth of the race, they may not be able to win it. Similarly, Senators have to keep in mind that they have six years to accomplish their goals instead of two. It means that they have a longer time frame to meet their goals and campaign promises. If they fail to accomplish anything meaningful the first year, there is more time to reach those goals over their current term. This in effect encourages greater stability, and possibly as the Constitution framers intended, may be less reactive to populist whims.

FIGURE 7.7 *Babymouse: Dragonslayer*
Source: Jennifer Holm and Matthew Holm, *Babymouse: Dragonslayer* (New York: Random House, 2009), pp. 68–69.

Challenging students to imagine a good simile or metaphor to represent what they want to talk about, therefore, is a great prewriting strategy. Thinking in metaphors, however, is often challenging for students, especially the younger ones. The more they're exposed to metaphors and similes, and the more they can think visually, the easier this will become. In a moment, we will present several brain dump ideas to give students practice in writing nonfiction using imagery.

Before proceeding to the brain dumps, however, you may want to present the image in Figure 7.6 for your students to better understand the use of visual imagery. For younger students, or even as a follow-up for older students, you may want to use the image from *Babymouse: Dragonslayer* displayed in Figure 7.7 to relay metaphor and visual imagery. It depicts Babymouse preparing to slay the math dragon that has haunted her for the entire book. We see Babymouse working math problems at her desk, and then putting on her armor consisting of simple math symbols to tackle any math problem.

Here are a few other visual metaphor possibilities:

- Balancing power and a ticking time bomb. *The United States Constitution: A Graphic Adaptation*, by Jonathan Hennessey and Aaron McConnell (p. 30), brilliantly depicts the pressure the framers felt when drafting the Constitution, as there were so many arguments (balance of power, slavery, proportional representation, who would be eligible to vote, and so on.).

- Feeling alone as if in a personal impermeable bubble. Depicted in *El Deafo* by Cece Bell (p. 47).

- Seeing oneself and another person having a conversation underwater. In *El Deafo* (p. 24), this depicts what speech sounds like to someone who is legally deaf.

- Waking up from a black-and-white dream to a colorful world – going to a new setting with a vast array of new and unusual animals. Depicted in *Last of the SandWalkers* by Jay Hosler (p. 99).

Here are some brain dumps you may want to give students to help them with imagery and metaphor in their writing:

- What animals, places, and things are you most like? Why?

- How is your relationship with some person like a battle? Explain what kind of battle it is.

- What is the stinkiest smell you can find? What does it remind you of? Write about the time you smelled that smell.

- What is the "most orange" emotion you can think of? Why? Do this with other colors.

- Who is the George Washington of a sports team? Write about the time that person most reminded you of George Washington. (Feel free to replace George Washington with other historical figures.)

- What song best describes your morning routine?

- What "dragons" have you slain last year? Describe the most difficult dragon.

Thus far, we've laid out strategies and tips for using graphic novels to help students learn skills for writing prose fiction and nonfiction. We've started with tips for writing prose, largely because your students will be more frequently assessed based on their prose writing. However, writing a comic strip is a different experience; in the next section we point out both how it is different while providing you with strategies to adjust.

Writing Graphic Novels

In this section we focus on teaching students to create graphic novels. One of the challenges when it comes to teaching students to write graphic novels is that many don't know how to brainstorm, to prewrite, or even to write the stories in this format. We address these issues in this section, providing guidelines and resources for brainstorming and for writing graphic novels. If you still feel a bit uncomfortable or unfamiliar with this format, we suggest you take some time to look through the following resources (see the Bonus Resource for details):

- Scott McCloud, *Making Comics* (grades 5+)

- Scott McCloud, *Understanding Comics* (grades 5+)

- James Sturm, Andrew Arnold, and Alexis Frederick-Frost, *Adventures in Cartooning* (series; grades 1–4)

- Neill Cameron, *How to Make Awesome Comics* (grades 2–5)

Brainstorming and Prewriting

In the brainstorming and prewriting process, students will need to decide what they are going to relay in images, what they will relay through narrative, and what they will relay through dialogue. In any prewriting process, the greater the effort put into prewriting, the better conceived the piece will be, and this will, hopefully, lead to an easier writing process.

When writing prose, there are several ways to brainstorm and plan out what's going to be written. For example, you can use a traditional outline or plot mountain. These tools will similarly be useful with graphic novels, but they don't help students plan the images they want to include. Toward that end, we offer two different approaches students can take when planning their graphic novel panels:

- Storyboarding.

- The comic script.

Each of these brainstorming tools has its strengths and weaknesses, and we make note of them.

Storyboarding

Storyboarding is often used when planning films, television shows, commercials, or graphic novels. Simply put, storyboarding entails creating sequences of drawings, or thumbnails, typically with some directions and dialogue underneath each thumbnail, representing the different shots or images planned for a final product. When used for a graphic novel, each thumbnail represents a single panel. A blank storyboard looks something like the graphic shown here.

Note: This Storyboard Worksheet can be found in a reproducible format on our websites (www.wiley.com/go/worthathousandwords, meryljaffe.com, and taliahurwich.com)

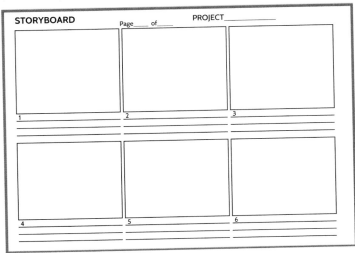

The purpose of using thumbnails is to visually lay out what everything will look like and how it will flow. For example, a series of thumbnails may show a writer whether the panels are sequenced in a clear way (as we saw in the sequencing lesson earlier in this chapter) and whether they look dynamic and engaging. Thumbnails also give students a chance to begin practicing how the characters look in different positions, making for (hopefully) fewer mistakes when they begin the writing process.

Further benefits of using storyboards in the prewriting process are that you and your students will get a better sense of what challenges lie ahead when they actually begin creating their graphic novel. For example, you can get a sense of how long it might take students to draw a panel – a detail that is immensely important as the writing process unfolds. If you look online, there are many different websites that help you create thumbnails. If you'd like, feel free to browse through these websites and have your students use them as they brainstorm. Here are a few resources you might want to check out:

- StoryBoard Pro (www.toonboom.com/products/storyboardpro) is designed to give teachers, students, and home-movie makers the tools they need to plan, plot, and create video (or graphic novel) projects. It guides users on selecting shot types; on importing video, still pictures, and sound clips; on how to create, save, and import templates; and on how to print blank storyboard worksheets for brainstorming ideas.

- Storyboard Fountain, for the Mac (storyboardfountain.com), focuses on going from script to visuals.

- StoryboardThat (www.storyboardthat.com) offers special versions for teachers and classroom use with a 14-day free trial.

- Canva – storyboards (www.canva.com/create/storyboards), scroll down the opening page and it tells you how to build your storyboard in five simple steps.

The challenge in using storyboards is that storyboarding can be time and work intensive. You need to make sure that students realize that these are sketches and as a result don't need to be perfect. At the same time, you want to make sure that students are taking each thumbnail fairly seriously: the more detail they put into the thumbnail, the clearer their panels are going to be. We recommend that, as you monitor your students' prewriting process, you try to ascertain which students need to spend more time with the thumbnails and which students need to spend less time.

In short, if your class has the time, storyboarding is potentially the most effective prewriting strategy for graphic novels. However, you may not have a lot of time to prewrite. Therefore, an alternative strategy is prewriting using a script.

Scripting

When using scripting to prewrite, students are asked to imagine what each panel will look like but are not asked to actually sketch the panels. The format used in this type of scripting is a bit different from what is generally imagined for a script. The script example given later in this section illustrates this format.

When using this scripting format, it's important that students think not only about what they want each panel to look like but also whether they are confident that they can draw that scene. For example, if they write in their script that a panel will include a chainsaw-juggling chinchilla, the students should be certain that they can draw a chinchilla juggling chainsaws. As you look over their work and you notice a panel that you think may be particularly challenging to draw, encourage your students to draft that one specifically and, if necessary, edit their script if they aren't happy with how their draft panel looks.

It is also important to recognize that each author has his or her own distinct way of writing a script. Some (especially if someone else is illustrating) may give a lot of detail; some may provide little detail.

The ultimate challenge when using a script is that you don't get to see how it works or how the panels fit or don't fit together on a given page. For first-time illustrators this can be problematic, as they have less feel regarding the pace than experienced authors do and less sense of whether in fact what they propose can actually be drawn.

The following example shows what a graphic novel script may look like. Titled "Dramatic Reading," it was written by Meryl Jaffe and illustrated by Janet Lee as a one-page story for the Comic Book Legal Defense Fund's annual fundraiser *Liberty Annual* – an anthology of short stories around the value of the First Amendment to the US Constitution.

DRAMATIC READING: MARY SHELLEY VS. THE CENSORS

by Meryl Jaffe and Janet Lee

Panel 1

Mary Shelley is sitting in front of an audience – kids and adults, reading an excerpt from her book, *Frankenstein*. This is a bit of a side view so we see only part of the room: Behind Shelley is a bookshelf filled with books, and the wall to our right, with a mural. We also see Shelley and some of the audience from the side.

The audience is sitting at the edge of their seats, focused on the story, invested, interested. The room lights are dimmed. Adding affect, there are candelabras lit on two side tables, one on each side of her. One of the side tables also has an old light up globe (yellowed with age). Their lights flicker as she reads, but her face remains highlighted. Behind her is a bookcases filled with books. . . .

To the side of Mary Shelley is a large wall mural of famous storybook characters that might include: Alice in Wonderland, Frankenstein, Dracula, the Three Musketeers, Dragons, Witches, King Arthur and Sir Lancelot, Wild Things, Dapper Men. . . .

Shelley is reading the following passage:

> *Mary Shelley:* I spent days and nights studying bodies degraded and wasted. I saw how the worm inherited the wonders of the eye and brain. . . . And in the midst of darkness, a sudden light broke upon me – a light so brilliant and wondrous, I became dizzy with the prospect. . . . I alone had succeeded in discovering the cause of reanimation, of rebirth . . . OF LIFE!! . . . I would make a being of gigantic stature. A new species would bless me as its creator. . . . But now that I had finished, the beauty of the dream vanished, and breathless horror and disgust filled my heart. . . . I beheld

(continued)

the wretch. His jaw opened and he muttered inarticulate sounds, while a grin wrinkled on his cheeks. GREAT GOD!

Panel 2

Three animated cartoon censors rush into the room from the back of the room – nearing the front of the room with Shelley and the bookcase. Behind them are huge dust clouds in their wake. (Many in the audience are coughing/choking from the dust.)

Mary Shelley isn't quite sure what's going on and has a shocked/befuddled expression. Her book is now hanging down to her side in one hand as she's clearly distracted and has stopped reading.

One censor has a large pink eraser in one hand and a black indelible marker in the other. The second censor has a large broom and bucket attached to an even larger ladder slung over his hunched back. The third censor enters last with rolls of stickers hanging off of his arms (one roll says "blasphemy," "racism, "language," "sexual content," "violence," "inappropriate," and "JUST WRONG").

These censors are shouting:

Censor 1: "No, no, no . . ."

Censor 2: "This will not do. . . . There are kids in the audience!"

Censor 3: "Not on my watch . . . oh no!"

You can see what the first three panels eventually looked like in Figure 7.8.

We leave the choice of whether to storyboard or to script to you and/or your students. Whichever you select, once the storyboard or script is done, it must be translated into the final product. These products can be created by hand, or you and your students can use apps and websites to create your graphic novels (see Appendix B for a complete list of apps and websites). Feel free to check these digital resources out before bringing them into your classroom.

Writing and Editing

As graphic novels become more widely used in classrooms and read in and outside the home, writing conventions unique to the medium will arise and be challenged. As always, it's important to know when to encourage students to experiment with challenging conventions (i.e. practices given as rules). Here are several conventions we have found in graphic novels.

Show, Don't Tell

Dialogue and text boxes should be used to complement images (as opposed to summarizing or repeating them). As a result, text can be used fairly sparingly in each panel. Don't write something that can be discerned from the image. If any panel has a lot of words on it, you should immediately be skeptical of whether all those words are actually needed in that panel.

FIGURE 7.8 "Dramatic Reading: Mary Shelley vs. the Censors"
Source: Meryl Jaffe and Janet Lee, "Dramatic Reading: Mary Shelley vs. the Censors," in Lauren Sankovitch (Ed.), *CBLDF Liberty Annual 2012* (Portland, OR: Image Comics, 2012), p.1.

Use an Establishing Shot

This is a convention also found in film and television. Often, you want to open a story with a panel that shows a lot of the setting to give the reader a sense of where the story is located. Then, the writer zooms in to give the reader a closer look at the characters – their intentions, their feelings, and/or their reactions. Establishing shots are sometimes also used to transition readers to new settings or to highlight pivotal moments in the plot.

Know When Not to Include Background or Setting

We've spoken about how the setting can be important. That said, sometimes writers will want to exclude the background entirely. When they do that, it's often because an action or reaction is so important that they want the reader's complete attention on it. Furthermore, coloring a blank background a specific color will also help set the tone. A completely red background will highlight anger or danger, while a completely yellow one will highlight joy. To provide another example: if the setting is generally bright, detailed, and/or colorful, a black background will add a significant amount of drama. In short, if a panel features high emotions that the writer wants to focus on, changing the background to a single color or removing the background entirely can highlight that moment.

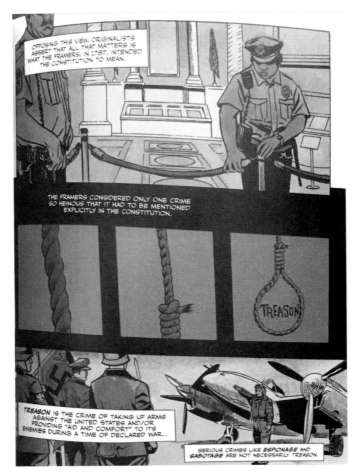

FIGURE 7.9 The United States Constitution: A Graphic Adaptation
Source: Jonathan Hennessey and Aaron McConnell, *The United States Constitution: A Graphic Adaptation* (New York: Hill & Wang, 2008), p. 73.

An example can be found in Figure 7.9, taken from Hennessey and McConnell's *The United States Constitution: A Graphic Adaptation*. These creators provide a lot of details in the backgrounds of the first and third panels, and a social studies teacher can spark a conversation as to why they chose to use a courtroom or an aviation pilot during the Second World War to make their point. However, the second panel, with a simple black and red background, sets a tone, sending a very clear message of the gravity of treason, which is only further drawn out by simply putting a noose in the foreground.

GRAPHIC NOVELS AND CONTENT-AREA CURRICULUM

One thing that's particularly exciting to see in educational research and at professional conferences is that educators are increasingly using graphic novels not only in language arts but across content areas. Even more encouraging is that they report positive results, from increased motivation and engagement to greater student incorporation of complex concepts. It is therefore our intent in this chapter to open up a dialogue that content-area teachers can have with language arts teachers. We hope that bridging the interdisciplinary gap can add life across classrooms and subjects. Furthermore, while this books is primarily for educators teaching reading and writing in grades 2 through 9, we recognize that many of you, especially in the younger grades, teach math, social studies, and science as well. So regardless of whether you teach across content areas or simply hope to expand conversations with colleagues across the curriculum, we conclude this book by discussing why graphic novels are viable content-area curricula choices and demonstrating how they can be integrated and used in unit lessons in a variety of ways.

Reasons for Using Graphic Novels in Your Math Classroom

Reason #1: Training Students to Successfully Read Word Problems

We'd like to open our discussion with the following math problem:

> An art teacher had ⅔ gallon of paint to pour into containers. If he poured ⅛ gallon of paint into each container until he ran out of paint, how many containers had paint in them, including the one that was partially filled?
>
> A. 1
>
> B. 3

C. 5

D. 6

This problem, a released question from the 2016 New York State Grade 6 Mathematics Test, requires many skills beyond basic or advanced math competency. Students need to do several things when reading a problem like this:

- First, students need to understand what is going on in the problem. In this particular case, an art teacher is emptying ⅔ gallon of paint into smaller ⅛ gallon containers.

- Then, students need to determine what the question is asking them – how many (⅛ gallon) containers the teacher will fill when pouring out the paint (⅔ gallon).

- Finally, students will then need to identify three more things: the important values they will need to manipulate, the basic mathematical functions they will need to do, and the proper order in which to do them. In this case, they will need to divide ⅔ by ⅛ and round up.

In short, being able to answer a question like the one posed here requires careful analytic reading skills paired with math competency as well as problem-solving skills. Some students enjoy solving puzzles, and will more likely do well in math as a result. Others will be confused, frustrated, and may very well give up. For those students, we need to get them to slow down enough to understand what they're reading as well as teaching them math competency.

One way that graphic novels can help is that graphic novels can be used to illustrate and decode math word problems. This added step does several things to help your students. First, it makes the scenario described in the question more concrete and understandable, and if the student gets confused, he or she can refer back to the illustrations to regain whatever clarity is needed. Second, it gives the students some time to process the question without having to worry about the math. Finally and hopefully, it makes the problem more fun to solve, thereby motivating your students.

In the following sample lesson, we demonstrate how we would use the graphic novel format to help train students to solve word problems such as the one we shared with you at the start of the chapter.

LESSON: USING GRAPHIC NOVELS TO DECONSTRUCT WORD PROBLEMS

As noted earlier, the following lesson uses a released question from the 2016 New York State Grade 6 Mathematics Test (nysed-prod.engageny.org/resource/released-2016-3-8-ela-and-mathematics-state-test-questions) and specifically covers dividing fractions. Feel free to choose a similar question appropriate for your grade level and math unit.

Mastery Objectives

◙ Students will be able to make sense of word problems and persevere in solving them.

◙ Students will be able make sense of abstract quantities by making elements of the word problem less abstract.

Materials Needed

The word problem introduced at the beginning of this chapter or a grade-appropriate word problem (to be used during guided practice), along with several other word problems (to be used during independent practice).

Introducing the Lesson

◙ Review fractions with your students.

◙ Make sure students know and can refer to notes that will help them do basic mathematics with fractions (add, subtract, multiply, and divide).

◙ *Do not explicitly tell them that they will need to divide fractions*. Ideally, students will be able to figure this out – first with help from you and ultimately without your help.

Guided Practice

Hand out and read the word problem you have selected.

As a class, plan and sketch a comic strip that illustrates what is happening in this word problem. You might create this strip using the following layout:

◙ *Panel 1* shows a stick figure art teacher with a bucket. The teacher is smiling and saying "OMG!" and the bucket says "Paint – 2/3 gallon."

◙ *Panel 2* shows the stick figure art teacher pouring the paint into a smaller container. The teacher has his or her brows furrowed (i.e. v-shaped eyebrows or with one hand is scratching his or her head) from concentration, and the smaller container has the label "1/8 gallon."

◙ *Panel 3* shows the art teacher pouring paint into another container next to the container shown in panel 2. The teacher has the v-shaped furrowed eyebrows and two drops of sweat. The second container also has the label "1/8 gallon."

◙ *Panel 4* has in large words "AND SO ON!" and has some background design that is fun (polka dots, zigzags, plain shading – something to signify that you're having some fun creating your comic strip).

◙ *Panel 5* has a confused teacher looking at a sea of containers. The teacher has several question marks floating above his or her head and is saying, "Wait . . . how many of these containers have paint again???"

(continued)

- Once the students understand the events as they unfold, discuss them and ask the students what mathematical function can be used to answer the question. Students should eventually come to realize that the painter is *dividing* the 2/3 gallon of paint into 1/8 gallon containers, requiring them to divide 2/3 by 1/8 and, if there's a remainder, add 1.

- Instruct students to refer to their notes, as mentioned in this lesson's introduction, and quickly review how to divide fractions before moving on.

- Answer the question (the correct answer is D, 6).

Independent Practice

Give students several word problems that use fractions to work on independently or in groups. Instruct students to create comic strips showing what is happening in each word problem to help them determine what math functions they will need to do in order to solve the word problem. Emphasize that these comic strips can be quick sketches – the point is to quickly illustrate what is happening, and not to have a publishable comic strip.

Debrief and Assessment

Discuss with students the importance of understanding what actions are happening in the word problem in order to understand what math skills they will need to use in order to solve the problem. Have students share how they figured out what math functions they needed based on their comics.

Assess students based on their ability to understand the narrative presented in the word problem as well as their ability to get the correct answer.

Reason #2: Addressing Standardized Requirements

Math is often challenging to teach because of the depth and breadth of skills it often requires. Math competency requires memorization (of basic facts, formulas, principles, and tables) and it requires practice. It requires a fluency in language and the ability to tease out information relevant to solving any given problem. It also requires students to have the ability to convert abstractions into visual models or already memorized equations, or to use more than one mathematical model and formula in order to solve a problem.

Then, of course, there are the math standards or general goals and practices we all need to incorporate. Whether following Common Core Standards or not, when teaching math we need to make sure our students can

- decode and make sense of the math problem;

- brainstorm possible solutions;

- express why those possible solutions are viable;

- know how to read, create, and use graphs, charts, tables, equations, and diagrams;

- understand and map relationships of numbers, expressions, equations, and formulas;

- recognize the tools they'll need to effectively engage those solutions; and

- understand and recognize various math symbols, properties, and equations necessary for solving the everyday and the less commonplace math problems they'll encounter.

This is a tall order for both teachers and students, and it is compounded for the math-phobic. Graphic novels, however, can help. They can motivate; they can reinforce many of the mathematical practices discussed here; they can be used to posit real-life, meaningful challenges that can be solved with math; and they can be used as a tool to slow down students' reading of a problem to ensure a more sophisticated mathematical literacy.

In the following sample lesson, we present one way a teacher can use graphic novels to teach geometry and fractions or percentages. One reason graphic novels lend themselves to geometry lessons is that their creators intentionally vary the number, size, and shape of the panels. They do this because the diversity of panel shapes per page engages readers (keeping things different and interesting), sets the storytelling pace, and relays overviews or specific detailed information. Even when only rectangles and squares are used (as they are the predominant shape of choice), their size and orientation (i.e. horizontal or vertical) vary. As such, the rectangles may be more square at times, more elongated at times, or taller, shorter, wider, narrower, and so on. And to help with pacing and storytelling, a trapezoid, triangle, or circle may be interspersed to show great action or instability, to show greater inclusion, or to help focus the reader's eye on a particular object, emotion, or action.

LESSON: USING GRAPHIC NOVELS TO REVIEW GEOMETRY

Mastery Objectives

- Students will review the area equations for different figures (squares, rectangles, circles).

- Students will understand that the highest or widest shape does *not* always mean the shape with the largest area.

- Students will practice using a ruler.

- *Optional*. Students will practice setting up fractions/percentages.

Materials Needed

- A page from a graphic novel that has panels in several different shapes (ideally, a square, a rectangle, and a circle, or you may also be able to find an appropriate graphic novel that also uses triangles and trapezoids).

- Copies of Figure 8.1, which has various rectangular shapes. Or, depending on the level of challenge you want, choose a page from a different graphic novel – either one used elsewhere in this book or one that you have found for your students.

(continued)

Note: Figure 8.1 can be found in a reproducible format on our websites (www.wiley.com/go/worthathousandwords; meryljaffe.com; and taliahurwich.com)

☐ A ruler for each student.

FIGURE 8.1   Measuring Panels in *Rust: A Visitor in the Field*
Source: Royden Lepp, *Rust: A Visitor in the Field* (Los Angeles: Archaia. 2008) p. 131.

I predict the largest panel is _____ because _____.

I predict the smallest panel is _____ because _____.

After measuring them all, the largest panel is _____.

After measuring them all, the smallest panel is _____.

Introducing the Lesson

▪ Have students quickly share the different formulas for finding the area of various shapes. Write the formulas on the board as they share.

▪ *Optional*. Also quickly review how to create a fraction/percentage.

▪ Hand out copies of the graphic novel page you have selected, either Figure 8.1 or some other page, and tell students they'll be using the panels on that page to practice measuring area.

Guided Practice

Briefly discuss students' impression of the page layout: what panel looks like it's taking up the most space on the page? What panel seems to be taking up the smallest area? Have students write down their predictions and the rationales behind those predictions.

Tell students that they will be finding out which panel actually has the largest area and which panel has the smallest. As a class, they will find the area of the first panel together, and they will then work independently on the remaining panels.

Have students recognize the shape of the first panel and identify which formula and which dimensions (e.g., length, width, diameter) will be required. Using a ruler, measure the panel dimensions that will be required. *Note* that if students have not worked with decimals yet, be sure to round to the nearest whole number.

Calculate the area of the panel.

Optional. As a class, calculate what fraction/percentage of the page this first panel takes up. Together, measure the length and width of the page, and calculate the page's area. Using the panel's area and the page's area, create the necessary fraction/percentage.

Independent Practice

On their own, students calculate the areas of the other panels on the graphic novel page. (*Optional*. They can also calculate what fraction/percentage of the page's area each panel covers.) If there is a circle panel, have students estimate the circle's center.

Once students have measured each panel's area, have them return to their predictions and briefly write, as a follow-up, whether their predictions were correct or incorrect. If they were incorrect, have them consider what they might have overlooked as they were making those predictions.

Debrief and Assessment

Have students present and discuss their findings. Share which panel actually has the largest area and which has the smallest area, and compare those results to what students thought at the beginning of this lesson. Discuss how guessing areas based on "eyeballing" may or may not work to their advantage (because they have to take two dimensions into account, and what might at first appear larger may in fact be smaller). Assert the importance of having and using measurements when making conclusions about a shape's area. Assess your students based on the accuracy of their work and the insights found in their discussions.

Reasons for Using Graphic Novels in Your Social Studies Classroom

As social studies teachers, we all try to give our students an understanding and an appreciation of the communities, society, and nation we live in. To do this, we need to help them understand not only various institutions but also where all of us, our community, and our government institutions came from. By understanding the struggles our founding leaders wrestled with, the solutions they found, and the challenges faced as a result of those solutions, students will be better equipped to face more modern challenges.

Moreover, understanding local or even national issues of citizenship and governance isn't enough anymore. In our ever-expanding world, where communication across immense land and water masses takes a matter of seconds, and in classrooms with increasingly diverse students whose roots can be traced across the globe, we need to understand the other nations and cultures we share our planet with. Whether considering interacting for social, professional, or political purposes, we need to recognize and understand that others have different languages, cultures, customs, and values, and learn how best to communicate, whether those differences are minor or major. In short, our students must learn not only about the immediate world around them but about the world at large. And as parents and educators, we help them do this through the books we have them read and through our social studies curricula. More specifically, when teaching social studies our goals are to teach them

- historical events;
- culture and cultural diversity;
- continuity and change among and between cultures;
- national and community institutions;
- the powers and challenges of governance;
- citizenship and civic ideals and practices; and
- global connections.

Graphic novels have a special place in social studies classrooms in part because they so deftly make their material come alive. The main characters look at us and invite us into their stories. We can feel (and therefore relate) to their challenges more closely – even if and when they appear to be so different from our own. As historical (and fictional) characters look at us and invite us into an event from time past or a location distant in time or place, we readers can more easily relate to what was seen, felt, and experienced then or there. Furthermore, graphic novels can relay simultaneous incidents and abstract concepts more effectively than simple prose alone can.

In "Why I Write Graphic Nonfiction: Teaching History Through Comics," a 2017 article for *Signature* online, Jonathan Hennessey (the author of five nonfiction graphic novels, including *The United States Constitution: A Graphic Adaptation*), discusses the appeal of teaching history via comics and the challenges he faced as a graphic novel author in representing very abstract concepts, such as the three-fifths compromise, and his effort to make these concepts more concrete and relatable. He reflects upon the challenges of teaching the Constitution, noting that "its sometimes anachronistic language . . . and abstract concepts like federalism, popular sovereignty, and the doctrine of incorporation pose high hurdles for any would-be [graphic novel] adapter to jump." Describing the specific challenge of depicting the three-fifths compromise, a highly abstract solution to an anachronistic problem, Hennessey discusses his solution of "positing slavery-era African Americans drawn as dehumanized walking abstractions – their bodies vertically vivisected just past the spines" (as shown in Figure 8.2).

FIGURE 8.2 Depiction of the Three-Fifths Compromise in *The United States Constitution: A Graphic Adaptation*
Source: Jonathan Hennessey and Aaron McConnell, *The United States Constitution: A Graphic Adaptation* (New York: Hill & Wang, 2008), p. 31.

Worth a Thousand Words

Looking at Hennessey's visual depiction (Figure 8.2), what is striking is not only how elegantly he explains the compromise, but also that he allows the image itself to share a powerful (and editorial) message. First, it makes us stop to try to figure out what's going on – why are those vertical lines superimposed going down the image. And in making us stop, Hennessey makes us think about several things. First, we have to think about the historical context that led to such a compromise. Second, Hennessey encourages us to think about the absurdity of the compromise and how or why anyone would want to count only three fifths of a person. Finally, Hennessey asks us to consider why this was such a contentious issue when the Constitution was written, and how these contentious issues have changed or remained the same to this day.

Here is just a sampling of our favorite nonfiction and historical fiction graphic novels. They are all listed in the Bonus Resource as well, and we ask that you refer to that resource for general details. Here, we note in parentheses following the titles the various social studies standards they teach and reinforce.

Alexander Hamilton, by Jonathan Hennessey and Aaron McConnell (historical events; culture and cultural diversity; continuity and change among and between cultures; national and community institutions; the powers and challenges of governance; citizenship and civic ideals and practices; and global connections).

American Born Chinese, by Gene Luen Yang (culture and diversity; and global connections).

Boxers and Saints, by Gene Luen Yang (historical events, culture and diversity; national and community institutions; the powers and challenges of governance; citizenship and civic ideals and practices; and global connections).

Brazen: Rebel Ladies Who Rocked the World, by Penelope Bagieu (historical events; culture and cultural diversity; continuity and change among and between cultures; national and community institutions; citizenship and civic ideals and practices; and global connections). Also note that there is some mature content dealing with torture.

Journey into Mohawk Country, by Van den Bogaert and George O'Connor (historical events; culture and cultural diversity; continuity and change among and between cultures; national and community institutions; the powers and challenges of governance; citizenship and civic ideals and practices; and global connections).

Laika, by Nick Abadzis (historical events; culture and cultural diversity; continuity and change among and between cultures; national and community institutions; the powers and challenges of governance; citizenship and civic ideals and practices; and global connections).

Lewis & Clark, by Nick Bertozzi (historical events; culture and cultural diversity; continuity and change among and between cultures; national and community institutions; the powers and challenges of governance; citizenship and civic ideals and practices; and global connections).

Little White Duck: A Childhood in China, by Na Liu and Andres Vera Martinez (historical events; culture and cultural diversity; continuity and change among and between cultures;

the powers and challenges of governance; citizenship and civic ideals and practices; and global connections).

Nathan Hale's Hazardous Tales, a series by Nathan Hale (historical events; culture and cultural diversity; continuity and change among and between cultures; national and community institutions; the powers and challenges of governance; citizenship and civic ideals and practices; and global connections).

Northwest Passage, by Scott Chantler (historical events; culture and cultural diversity; continuity and change among and between cultures; national and community institutions; the powers and challenges of governance; citizenship and civic ideals and practices; and global connections).

Resistance by Carla Jablonski and Leland Purvis (historical events; culture and cultural diversity; continuity and change among and between cultures; the powers and challenges of governance; citizenship and civic ideals and practices; and global connections).

Satchel Paige: Striking Out Jim Crow, by James Sturm and Rich Tommaso (historical events; culture and cultural diversity; continuity and change among and between cultures; the powers and challenges of governance; citizenship and civic ideals and practices). Also note that there is an introduction by Gerald Early, noted essayist, author, American culture critic, and director of the Center for Humanities at Washington University in St. Louis, along with notes in the back of the book about specific panels, with historical facts and details relating to those panels.

Soupy Leaves Home, by Cecil Castellucci and Jose Pimienta (culture and cultural diversity; continuity and change among and between cultures; the powers and challenges of governance; and citizenship and civic ideals and practices). This historical fiction offers footnotes containing facts and reference details about hoboes and what life was like in Depression-era United States.

The Gettysburg Address: A Graphic Adaptation, by Jonathan Hennessey and Aaron McConnell (historical events; culture and cultural diversity; continuity and change among and between cultures; national and community institutions; the powers and challenges of governance; and citizenship and civic ideals and practices).

The Silence of My Friends, by Mark Long, Jim Demonakos, and Nate Powell (historical events; culture and cultural diversity; continuity and change among and between cultures; national and community institutions; the powers and challenges of governance; and citizenship and civic ideals and practices).

The United States Constitution: A Graphic Adaptation, by Jonathan Hennessey and Aaron McConnell (historical events; culture and cultural diversity; national and community institutions; the powers and challenges of governance; citizenship and civic ideals and practices; and global connections).

They Changed the World: Crick & Watson, by Lewis Helfand and Naresh Kumar (historical events; national and community institutions; the powers and challenges of governance; citizenship and civic ideals and practices; and global connections).

Trinity: A Graphic History of the First Atomic Bomb, by Jonathan Fetter-Vorm (historical events; national and community institutions; the powers and challenges of governance; citizenship and civic ideals and practices; and global connections).

In the next lesson, we model one example of how you might incorporate nonfiction and/or historical fiction graphic novels into your social studies curriculum. Note that in our model lesson we leave you the option of using graphic novels as primary texts, support texts, or anchor texts. We begin the lesson with students reading graphic novels and offer you links with additional resources and primary texts. For more titles and lesson suggestions, please visit our website.

LESSON: USING GRAPHIC NOVELS TO EXPLORE CITIZENSHIP (JIGSAW ACTIVITY)

Mastery Objective. Students will explore what *citizenship* means and how that meaning may vary from culture to culture or within one culture from era to era.

Materials Needed

An assortment of graphic novels that relay or present citizenship in different ways. In selecting these books, keep these notes in mind:

- Our list of some of our favorite nonfiction and historical fiction graphic novels earlier in this chapter indicates which general social studies themes each book addresses.

- You'll find a more extensive list of options in the Bonus Resource, along with a summary of each book. You may want to use these summaries to introduce your chosen books to your students before they read them.

Introducing the Lesson

- With the class, create a working definition for the concept of *citizenship*, and for what being a good or model citizen might look like.

- Once a definition is established, tell students that they will be reading a number of different books (either in groups or individually, based on your decision and available resources), each relaying aspects of good or poor citizenship. Students will be responsible for discussing how citizenship was relayed in their book(s) and how well the class's working definition of citizenship held up, making sure to explain why it did or did not hold up.

- *Optional.* Ask students if there is anything they might want to add, delete, or change to their working definitions before they hit the books.

Independent or Group Practice

Divide your class into groups – one for each book you've chosen for them to read. Have them read the book (for homework or during class), and then meet in their respective groups to discuss how it relays citizenship. Have them complete these activities:

- Create a working definition of what constitutes good or poor citizenship, based on the story or content of the book.

- Generate their own guidelines for determining how their definition does and/or does not fit the class definition and why that might be.

- *Optional.* Have them create a poster board that depicts and illustrates good citizenship, based on the book they read.

Guided Practice (a whole class activity)

Have each group present how their book relays good or poor citizenship.

Have them discuss how and why their book's rendering of good citizenship does or does not differ from the class definition.

Once groups finish their presentations, discuss how and why the group definitions may or may not vary from the original class definition.

Optional. Present or have the students read or listen to one or more of these additional resources on citizenship:

- "What the Constitution Says About Citizenship," *Scholastic Teacher's Guide* (www.scholastic .com/teachers/articles/teaching-content/what-constitution-says-about-citizenship).

- "Teaching Good Citizenship's Five Themes," *Education World* (www.educationworld .com/a_curr/curr008.shtml).

- "The Meaning of U.S. Citizenship," *Los Angeles Times*, October 4, 2014 (www.latimes .com/nation/la-ed-citizenship-part-1-20141005-story.html).

- "Video Series: What Does Citizenship Mean to You?" *Los Angeles Times*, November 24, 2014 (graphics.latimes.com/la-ed-citizenship).

- Michel Martin, "A Conversation About What It Means to Be a Good Citizen," transcript from *All Things Considered*, National Public Radio, June 10, 2017 (www.npr .org/2017/06/10/532400363/a-conversation-about-what-it-means-to-be-a-good-citizen).

Optional. Discuss what a model citizen might have looked like in your town in 1776? How might this have changed over time, and why or why not?

Optional. Discuss how this definition might change in a different culture or nation, and why or why not.

(continued)

Optional. Discuss what your students might do in and out of school to be good citizens.

Optional. Discuss what might happen if there were no rules or expectations of how to behave and interact at home, at school, on the bus, or on the street.

Debrief and Assessment

Evaluate students' poster boards if they made them, specifically considering their success in depicting and relaying important citizenship qualities. Discuss these qualities as depicted on the poster boards or in student discussions, and have students brainstorm ways they can serve their families and community.

Reasons for Using Graphic Novels in Your Science Classroom

Within our science classrooms our goals as educators are to get our students to think about the world around them and to better understand how things work, how objects and animals interact with each other, and how and what we can do to help save ourselves, our planet, and all the things we often take for granted but so deeply rely upon. Additionally, we want our students to think scientifically: to be able to pose a question based on observations, come up with a hypothesis about what the answer might be, and then test that hypothesis. More specifically, when teaching science our goals are to teach these areas:

- *Scientific inquiry* – understanding the rationale and skills needed.

- *Physical science* – focusing on facts, principles, theories, and models regarding the properties and structures of objects and materials.

- *Life science* – focusing on facts, principles, theories, and models relating the characteristics, functions and life cycles of living organisms and living systems.

- *Earth and space science* – focusing on facts, concepts, principles, theories, and models relating to the properties and structures of Earth and the solar system.

- *Science and technology* – helping students understand how scientific phenomena and advances in technology affect human life.

- *Science in personal and social perspectives* – helping students develop and act upon decisions regarding personal and community health and resources, changes in the environment, and natural hazards.

- *History and the nature of science* – using history to better understand the role science has played in the development of various cultures.

For reasons similar to those we presented in our discussion of graphic novels in the social studies classroom, graphic novels have a place in science classrooms as well. Their graphic-textual pairing makes content more memorable and meaningful and allows them to relay simultaneous incidents and abstract concepts more immediately and effectively than prose alone can do. Furthermore, within the field of science, researchers are finding that weak students, after engaging with graphic novels, are more likely to report having an increased "science identity"; that students remember more of the content they read in science comics and exhibit greater motivation to read science comics. Finally, the narrative structure used in graphic novels helps pique students' curiosity, leading them to ask questions – a first (and important) step in the scientific process.

Here are some of our favorite graphic novels for science content learning. They are all listed in the Bonus Resource with their general details. Here, we note the various science standards they teach and reinforce.

Around the World, by Matt Phelan (science as inquiry; science and technology standards; history and nature of science standards).

Big Bad Iron Clad!, in the Nathan Hale's Hazardous Tales series, by Nathan Hale (science as inquiry; physical science; science and technology; and history and the nature of science).

Dinosaurs: Fossils and Feathers, by M. K. Reed and Joe Flood (science as inquiry; life science; history and nature of science).

Flying Machines: How the Wright Brothers Soared, by Alison Wilgus and Molly Brooks (science as inquiry; science and technology; history and nature of science).

Howtoons: (Re)Ignition, by Fred Van Lente, Tom Fowler, and Jordie Bellair (science as inquiry; physical science; science and technology; science in personal and social perspectives; and history and the nature of science).

Howtoons: Tools of Mass Construction, by Dr. Saul Griffith, Nick Dragotta, Ingrid Dragotta, Arwen Griffith, Joost Bonsen, Jeff Parker, Warren Simons, Sandy Jarrel, Meredith McClaren, Jason Marzloff, Leigh B. Estabrooks, Lee Loughridge, Rich Starkings, Comicraft, Jimmy Betancourt, and Andrea Dunlap (science as inquiry; physical science; science and technology).

Last of the SandWalkers, by Jay Hosler (science as inquiry; physical science; life science; science and technology; and history and the nature of science).

Primates: The Fearless Science of Jane Goodall, Dian Fossey, and Biruté Galdikas, by Jim Ottaviani and Maris Wicks (science as inquiry; life science; and history and the nature of science).

Robots and Drones, by Mairghread Scott and Jacob Chabot (science as inquiry; physical science; science and technology; and history and the nature of science).

They Changed the World: Crick & Watson, by Lewis Helfand and Naresh Kuma (science as inquiry; life science; science and technology; and history and the nature of science).

Trinity: A Graphic History of the First Atomic Bomb, by Jonathan Fetter-Vorm (science as inquiry; physical science; science and technology; and history and the nature of science).

Xoc: The Journey of a Great White, by Matt Dembicki (science as inquiry; physical science; life science; and history and the nature of science).

With these book options and the reasons for incorporating graphic novels into science curricula, let's take a closer look through a sample lesson. In this lesson, we take *Xoc: The Journey of a Great White*, by Matt Dembicki, and show you how we might use it.

Xoc: The Journey of a Great White is an all-ages book that chronicles the life cycle of a female great white shark and her journey to give birth. Interestingly, it documents not only her journey (from the Farallon Islands, approximately 30 miles off the coast of San Francisco, to Maui – some 2000+ miles) but also how the lives of other species (including but not restricted to humans) interact with and impact upon her life. It deals with biological and environmental issues and is a very powerful story.

LESSON: USING GRAPHIC NOVELS TO LEARN ABOUT, RESEARCH, AND EXPLORE GREAT WHITE SHARKS (JIGSAW ACTIVITY; GRADES 4+)

Mastery Objective. Students will read, research, and construct what life is like for great white sharks, and how the world and people around them impact on their lives.

Materials Needed

Xoc: The Journey of a Great White, a graphic novel by Matt Dembicki.

Access to or copies of any combination of the following assorted additional resources:

- Shark Savers, an organization dedicated to saving sharks, has an excellent website (sharksavers.org) where you can find a variety of articles (the most recent are posted on the organization's home page) and information on these topics:

  - Shark biology (www.sharksavers.org/en/education/biology).

  - Why sharks are in trouble and why humans are the main culprits (the selling of shark cartilage and shark liver oil as cures for ailments and of shark fins as valuable seafood products, and recreational fishing, are just a few of the causes) (www.sharksavers.org/en/education/sharks-are-in-trouble).

  - Why sharks are important to us:

    - For ecotourism (www.sharksavers.org/en/education/the-value-of-sharks/sharks-and-ecotourism).

    - For their roles in balancing food webs and in keeping sea grass beds and other vital habitats healthy (www.sharksavers.org/en/education/the-value-of-sharks/sharks-role-in-the-ocean).

  - Studying sharks and shark research (www.sharksavers.org/en/education/sharks-and-people/shark-science).

- The Smithsonian Institute's "Ocean Portal: Great White Sharks," is an excellent resource about the life and evolution of sharks, research on them, the human and ecological impact sharks have and why they should be saved, and the threats sharks face (ocean.si.edu/ocean-life/sharks-rays/great-white-shark).

- The Florida Museum has a wonderful website chock-full of information on great white sharks, including their importance and danger to humans, geographical distribution around the world, habitat, distinguishing characteristics, social behavior, diets, and predators (www.floridamuseum.ufl.edu/fish/discover/species-profiles/carcharodon-carcharias).

- Facts about great white sharks from livescience.com (including size, habitat, habits, diet, conservation status, and more) (www.livescience.com/27338-great-white-sharks.html).

- The Shark Conservation Act, signed into law by President Obama on January 4, 2011:

  - Official link with a summary, history, and overview and a link to read each text version from the time the bill was introduced until it was signed into law (www.govtrack.us/congress/bills/111/hr81).

  - Summary and details posted by the Animal Welfare Institute (awionline.org/content/shark-conservation-act).

  - A detailed article about the Act, "Shark Conservation Act Becomes Law," by Brandon Keim for wired.com, also contains three excellent additional links to explore (www.wired.com/2011/01/shark-conservation-act).

- The article "Great White Shark Diet Is More Than Seals," by Brian Switek, *Wired: Science*, October 6, 2012 (www.wired.com/2012/10/great-white-shark-diet-is-more-than-seals).

- The article "Orcas Are Killing Great White Sharks and Eating Their Livers," by Douglas Main, Newsweek, May 10, 2017 (www.newsweek.com/orcas-killing-great-white-sharks-eating-livers-607002).

- The article "Life Cycle of a Shark," by Nicole Martinez, updated April 25, 2017, discusses fertilization and gestation, internal gestation, external incubation (for other shark species but not great whites), birth, growth, and adulthood (sciencing.com/life-cycle-shark-6723691.html).

- A National Geographic video on the challenges of photographing and learning firsthand about great white sharks (www.nationalgeographic.com/animals/fish/g/great-white-shark). And the related article, which integrates Hollywood's images (and misconceptions) with facts garnered, including facts from the video (www.nationalgeographic.com/magazine/2016/07/great-white-shark-research-population-behavior).

- National Geographic Kids, a website with general overview information including the size, speed, birth, and habitats of great whites (kids.nationalgeographic.com/animals/great-white-shark/#great-white-shark-surface.jpg).

(continued)

Introducing the Lesson

Introduce students to *Xoc: The Journey of a Great White*, by Matt Dembicki. Tell them that they will be studying the life of a great white shark and how the world and people around these sharks can impact upon their lives. Tell students that they will read the book (independently during class time and/or for homework), and then they will be divided into groups to research, explore, and then share how various environmental factors impact sharks' lives. Each group will be assigned a different environmental factor.

Guided Practice

After students have read *Xoc: The Journey of a Great White*, ask and discuss with them what they've learned from the book, recording their comments on the board. We suggest you record the information in categories analogous to the groups you will be dividing the students into: such as life cycle, diet, natural habitat, and threats sharks face.

Once your students seem to have exhausted the facts they picked up about great whites from the book, ask them what information they still need to learn in order to get a clearer, more detailed understanding of great white sharks – across each of the categories you've listed on the board.

After students have brainstormed what information they still need to know, break them into groups with the list or with copies of resources and links they'll need to collect the necessary information. Tell them that they will be presenting their facts to the class once their research is complete.

Optional. Have students find their own resources – possibly in a school or community library – and then have you approve them for their group work.

Independent or Group Practice

You may want to divide your students into the following groups:

- Life cycle
- Diet
- Natural habitat
- Threats sharks face

Each group will be responsible for

- an oral presentation with visual aids (such as poster boards, graphs, photographs and/or relevant video clips, or infographics – the choice is up to you or up to them); and
- a bibliography listing the resources they used.

Make sure to tell students how much time each group will be given for the presentation, so they can plan accordingly.

Guided Practice (a whole class activity)

Have each group present their material.

After each presentation, ask the group members to discuss what was easy and what was hard for them as they gathered related facts.

Ask them what they might do differently next time and why.

Debrief and Assessment

After the presentations ask students to share their favorite fact from any of the presentations other than theirs. Ask why it was their favorite fact. Then ask them what surprised them and why. Finally, ask them how learning about great white sharks has impacted on their lives and what (if anything) they might do or change as a result, particularly what they might do to help save the environment and valuable at-risk ecosystems.

Grade students on the depth, detail, and organization of their presentations; on the bibliographies they assembled; and on class comments and participation.

9

FINAL WORDS

Where We've Come From

Early on in this book, we noted how fragile the understanding of graphic novels' place in today's classrooms currently is. This book has been our effort to make graphic novels more understandable so teachers can better use them in their homes, libraries, and classrooms. Yet, partially because we're all only starting to think critically and deeply about graphic novels, we recognize that this is just the tip of the iceberg.

In the preceding pages, we've relayed some of the current concerns and benefits teachers face when considering graphic novels and integrating them into their classrooms. We have shared thoughts, arguments, and sample lessons detailing how to read graphic novels, how to teach reading them, and how to integrate them into language arts and content-area curricula. The appendixes that follow share tools that can further help you, and there is also an online companion to this book with an extensive list of graphic novels you can use. Ultimately, we posit that there is a distinct place graphic novels can have in modern classrooms, and that their inclusion will enrich students' education and literacy practices.

Where We're Heading

Looking to the future, the introduction of graphic novels into classrooms may serve two general purposes. First, their use in classrooms will empower educators to reach and encourage a wider community of readers. Their introduction also appears to have helped teachers to question educational goals, practices, and resources as they attempt to advance literacy and educational practices. For example:

- The integration of graphic novels into classrooms raises the question of what literacy is, and what literacy will look like in 20 years' time.

- The reading and use of graphic novels helps to raise the question of how innovative print media can be.

- Incorporating graphic novels into science classrooms raises the question of how interdisciplinary these traditionally siloed topics might become.

- Furthermore, the integration of graphic novels into our libraries and classrooms has helped teachers to question and push forward the dialogue surrounding classroom themes, goals, and resources.

Where We May Continue Together

This is where you come in. We hope that we've given you the tools to successfully advocate for and use graphic novels in your classroom. But beyond that, we hope we have started a dialogue with you – a dialogue we hope will continue. Toward this end, we would love to hear from you. We want to know what questions remain and what feedback you have to offer. We want to know the roadblocks that continue to stand before you. And just as important, we want to know your successes. It is only through professional dialogue that we can better understand this medium and what it can offer all of us and our students. So please stay in touch: meryljaffe.com and taliahurwich.com.

We wish you the best and thank you for the time spent with us.

APPENDIX A: GUIDELINES AND RESOURCES TO SUPPORT YOUR READING AND GRAPHIC NOVEL CHOICES

Getting Approval for Your Reading Selection Choices

1. **Review school and library policies** regarding reading selections. If your school or library doesn't have an explicit policy, you may want to work with colleagues to create one. If there is an outdated policy, review and update it. Be sure to include and relate the school's and the district's educational goals in this policy. In the long run, this will help to avert questions, challenges, and bans.

2. **Offer "parent education" programs and workshops** to introduce graphic novels. Choose wisely. Make sure to relay that there are outstanding kids' graphic novels that

   a. have been awarded prestigious literary awards such as the Newbery and Caldecott awards and the National Book Award;

   b. are getting starred reviews from *School Library Journal*, *Kirkus Reviews*, and *Horn Book Magazine*; and

   c. are found on "Best Reading" lists, including those in the American Library Association's *School Library Journal*.

3. **Be prepared**. Read the book from cover to cover to vet the book's appropriateness for your reader(s) and to prepare for any possible objections.

4. **Do research**. You may want to do a media and online search to see whether there have been issues or objections in the past about the book you want to use, as well as to see what, if any, objections have recently been raised about reading choices in your community. Furthermore, you may want to research awards and accolades garnered by the book you hope to use. Be prepared to tell stories or quote comments from parents and children about how the book has touched them.

5. **Know your audience** (which again is where having a school or library policy will be helpful). Make sure you understand both individual and community concerns and be prepared with responses to those concerns.

6. **Provide handouts** with information on relevant policies, statistics, and/or other relevant data or information.

7. **Find support** from colleagues, other parents, teachers, librarians, and/or administrators who can stand with you. Know also that there are organizations and resources set up to help you with just such challenges. We list them among the following resources.

For More Help, Please Refer to These Resources

- Freedom to Read Foundation (FTRF): www.ftrf.org

- American Library Association (ALA) Office for Intellectual Freedom (OIF), and *Intellectual Freedom and Censorship Q and A* (brochure): www.ala.org/advocacy/ intfreedom/censorshipfirstamendmentissues/ifcensorshipqanda

- National Council of Teachers of English (NCTE) Intellectual Freedom Center: www.ncte.org/action/anti-censorship

- NCTE, "The Student's Right to Read," a guideline: www.ncte.org/positions/statements/ righttoreadguideline

- NCTE, "Defining and Defending Instructional Methods": www.ncte.org/positions/ statements/defendinginstrmethod

- NCTE, "Guidelines for Selection of Materials in English Language Arts Programs" (dated 2014 – you may want to use this as a template for your own policies): www.ncte.org/positions/statements/material-selection-ela

- Comic Book Legal Defense Fund (CBLDF), *Resources*: cbldf.org/resources

APPENDIX B: RESOURCES FOR CREATING AND USING GRAPHIC NOVELS IN YOUR CLASSROOM

For Making Comics and Graphic Novels

Books That Explain the Process

- *The Drawing Lesson: A Graphic Novel That Teaches You How to Draw*, by Mark Crilley (Berkeley, CA: Watson-Guptill, 2016). This book takes kids and aspiring artists of all ages through a set of personal drawing lessons. It covers drawing what you see, shading, understanding light and shadow, checking proportions, and putting sketches and compositions together for a final product. (Grades 4+)

- *How to Make Awesome Comics*, by Neill Cameron (New York: Scholastic, 2017). Professor Panels and Art Monkey take young readers from brainstorming ideas to creating art and text to tell awesome stories about robots, pirates, monsters, heroes, and villains. They teach kids how to tell funny stories and dramatic stories. They even detail how to create awesome endings. (Grades 2–5)

- *Making Comics: Storytelling Secrets of Comics, Manga and Graphic Novels*, by Scott McCloud (New York: HarperCollins, 2006). This graphic novel details how to write with pictures and make choices about moment, frame, image, words, and the flow of panels. It also discusses helpful tools, techniques, and technologies as well as helping readers to understand different comic genres and styles. (Grades 6+)

- *Understanding Comics: The Invisible Art*, by Scott McCloud (New York: HarperCollins, 1993). This book (in graphic novel format) discusses the origins of comics, and then details the art of reading and understanding comics. It discusses different types of panels, text balloons, gutters, the use of line and texture to tell the story, the use of color, how the passage of time can be framed in comic panels, and the art of showing versus telling. (Grades 6+)

- *Will Eisner's Comics and Sequential Art: Principles and Practices from the Legendary Cartoonist*, by Will Eisner (New York: W. W. Norton, 1985, 2008). (Grades 10+)

Web Tools for Creating Comics and Graphic Novels

- PIXTON (web): www.pixton.com
- Comic Life (Mac or Windows): plasq.com/downloads/comic-life-desktop
- Comic Creator (Windows): summitsoft.com/products/comic-creator
- Clip Studio Paint (Manga Studio; Mac or Windows): my.smithmicro.com

For Creating Storyboards

- StoryBoard Pro (by Atomic Learning) is designed to give teachers, students, and home movie makers the tools they need to plan, plot, and create video (or graphic novel) projects. It guides users on selecting shot types; importing video, still pictures, and sound clips; creating, saving, and importing templates; and printing blank storyboard worksheets for brainstorming ideas: www.atomiclearning.com/k12/en/storyboardpro.
- Storyboard Fountain (Mac) focuses on going from script to visuals: storyboardfountain.com.
- StoryboardThat offers special versions for teachers and classroom use with a fourteen-day free trial: www.storyboardthat.com.
- Canva – scroll down the opening page and this site tells you how to build your storyboard in five simple steps: www.canva.com/create/storyboards.

Additional Links and Resources

- Visit our websites: meryljaffe.com and taliahurwich.com.
- For articles and web posts on how comics are beneficial in schools and classrooms, for classroom resources when using comics in the classroom, for suggested reading lists (pre-2009), and for additional tools, lesson plans, and more (pre-2009), please visit: www.teachingdegree.org/2009/07/05/comics-in-the-classroom-100-tips-tools-and-resources-for-teachers.
- The *School Library Journal*'s *Good Comics for Kids* is a collaborative blog covering kids' comics and written by a group of librarians, parents, and writers for readers to age 16: blogs.slj.com/goodcomicsforkids.
- "Using Graphic Novels in Education" is an online column written by Meryl and Talia. Each post takes a close look at one graphic novel, with a summary and overview of the book, a discussion of themes and age appropriateness, lesson suggestions, additional online links and resources, and paired reading suggestions: cbldf.org/using-graphic-novels-in-education.

INDEX